# Connecting with Your Angel

## ~ A Guide to your Guardian ~

~ Angelyn Joy ~
*2014*

Copyright © 2014 by Angelyn Joy, Whitby, ON Canada

All rights reserved.
This book or any portion thereof may not be reproduced or used in any manner whatsoever without the express written permission of the publisher except for the use of brief quotations in a book review or scholarly journal.
First Printing: 2014
Second Printing: 2015

ISBN 978-1-312-44497-3

## Dedication

*This book is dedicated to my wonderful daughter, Lenka. You are the inspiration in my life. Thank you for choosing me to be your mother. You are a beautiful, caring woman, and a blessing to me. I am so Proud of you! Words cannot express the feelings of Joy that you have brought into my life!! Love you to the MooN & BacK!*

*And to Janet T, Debbie F and RoseAnn W; you are beautiful Souls... thank you for all the help and insight you have given me. For the Courage to stick by my side and having the will to encourage me to complete this. You have shown me that 'true friendships' are never far away, no matter where you live in life...*

**~ *The Joys in my life; without you, who knows where I would be!!* ~**

# FORWARD

They say there are Angels among us. I've always hoped and believed that that was a possibility, but it does sound just a bit farfetched doesn't it?

I'm here to share with you what I know to be true about that statement. I met Angelyn Joy several years ago on the "Psychic Circuit". I was working for a vendor who did the same shows as Angelyn Joy did, we certainly were friendly and waved hello each day and shared small tidbits in the spirit of positivity, but we didn't really know each other.

My knowing that there is/was something special about this wonderful woman who had this childlike quality of unbridled joy didn't really hit until we decided to meet for dinner one evening before one of Angelyn's TV appearances.

As I sat there listening to her amazing story of the journey she's been on from childhood to the present, I realized that Angelyn Joy wasn't just a nomenclature for her – she was embracing the Archangel Radzekiel, that she channels. It (for want of a better term, because Angels are neither, male, or female) was a part of her, not just an entity that she channels at will.

That dinner of conversation and knowing was the beginning of a journey that we've shared closely ever since.

There were many times when Angelyn questioned her gifts – and I'm sure felt alone in the world because her gift ensured that she would always be different, and sometimes different is painful. That is part of her "Lesson in the Learning"©, to understand her journey, to learn to be open to receiving the messages from her Angels that she is meant to share – to embrace that "differentness" that truly sets her apart so that her gift can shine through.

I now see before me the butterfly-like transformation that has quietly unfolded within the depths of Angelyn Joy's Soul – her acceptance of her place in the here and now to help others understand a little better what their Life's Purpose is, to guide them to be the Highest and Best that they too can be. That is how Angelyn Joy best lives her Soul's Purpose.

Angelyn Joy has been my teacher – to be compassionate, tenacious, positive and to stand firm throughout adversity and embrace MY Soul's Purpose. That has been and continues to be her gift to me, and for that I AM so very grateful.

I hope you find within this book, the information, guidance and understanding that you are looking for to become the person you were meant to become. I know that that is the gift Angelyn Joy offers here.

*Namaste*

**RoseAnnWaters,**
*Change Catalyst, Transformation
Coach Success Vision ~ Coaching, Training, Consulting*

# Preface

When you are connecting with the 'Celestial Beings of Light'; you are never alone... An Angel once told me that every person I would meet along my path would be an essential part of creating the person I would become. For that, I am Grateful, seeing each of the experiences on my path as the Joy embracing all that which becomes me. There have been many people I have met in my travels, that; without consciousness have never really understood who I really was. I realize that this was a part of their path; if for only but a moment. Every expression of another has allowed me to feel and to recognize that part within me which has been hidden. I am allowed to re-open to these experiences and to grow from them. Those who neglected me, saw me as without integrity, never knew me, nor had taken the time to get to know me. I now realize this was a mirror of experience for them. And, albeit sometimes painful, this was a part of their integral growth, coinciding, sometimes colliding, with my own growth patterns. Life, is a series of mazes, much like a labyrinth, complete with its twists and turns; its laughter; its tears. I have learned to go deeper within myself to embrace that part of me which is real.

That part of my life which holds my own truths. That part of me, where life resides, creating my own experiences. Through this understanding, the Angels have been my only guidance; my light. Showing me sides of myself which may appear real, and the sides which really are in fact real. Now I share these words of guidance with you so that you may see that you are perfect; you are whole; you are complete - in every way.

~ *Angelyn* ~ (a.k.a: Archangel Radzekiel)

# *Introduction*

Living in today's society, social life is stressful, at the best of times. Many who are self-employed; single parents, or just single people trying to make their place in this world. We are all on the path searching for that which is us. Searching for that which is an extension of all that is; extensions of who we are, and connects the wholeness of our lives, with our true experiences.

Along with all of the stresses of the outside world, many of us feel very much alone. Many suffer from depression, anxiety and other disorders caused by undo stress which can further lead to physical disorders of the body. You are not alone, and you do not have to suffer the immense 'weight of the world' alone. You have an enormous entourage of beautiful Celestial Beings - Angels - to guide you, to protect you, and to open doors for you, but you must first 'ask' for help.

So then, what are these Celestial Beings designated to help us? Simply put, they are beings of Pure Love and Pure Light. As it has been told to me by the Almighty

Creator; an "Angel is to God what a ray of sunshine is to the Sun". Each Soul on this planet was assigned to an Angel. Angels are our leaders, our protectors; our teachers of Divine Guidance. These personal Guardians are with you through everything you endure in this lifetime and in every lifetime. They are your guide to life and to the afterlife. In total, there are Nine Choirs of Angels, the lowest being closest to the Earth, with the Highest, first order of angels, being closest to the Heavens, the Universe. You have access to all of them, at any time.

Your Guardian Angel is a gift to you from God; a light source higher than our own. The hardest part of what I do is tell my clients that their loved ones are not Angels, in fact they have a very 'special' role to us when they pass, and that is the role of a 'Spirit Guardian', a protector to us of a different kind. So you see we truly are not alone.

The Angels are here to help you with everything, but you must remember that no Angel will do all the work for you, and you must tie up any loose ends to reach the ultimate of your goals. You must set your intentions with purity of heart. You are meant to be the best that you can be. If you follow your Divine guidance (Angels), you will move toward being your best, your very best!

You are being moved, moment by moment, in the direction of spiritual consciousness, and as you progress to each new level of you own personal spiritual consciousness, you begin to let go of some self-limiting beliefs that have been imposed onto you by the human mind. Once balanced at this new level of consciousness you discover some other self-limiting beliefs which now must be 'let-go'. This is a lifelong journey; there is no rush. Patience on one's journey will allow you to experience your joy, every step of the way. Live each day to the fullest. Living life to the fullest means to live life with detachment from prejudice and bias, and with some discernment in order to fully feel the Love and acceptance that is available to you in every moment.

Angel guidance and Angel Therapy are tools available to you; delivered from the guidance of these Celestial Beings with their Purest Love and Purest Light. Everything which is revealed to you comes from the purest of Love and Light that only an Angel can give.

This shall not be altered in any way. Guidance is granted to you from your Guardian Angel, to help you with your healing, and your life journey. Angel Therapy reaches out to all Angels to help with healing and to harmonize your life in every possible way. Angel Therapy guides you to see clearly and enables you to receive Divine Guidance from both the Creator and all the Angels.

All Angels live and abide under the Universal Law, which states: *"No Angel shall interfere with a human's life; unless its life threatening (and it is not your time) ~ or ~ unless they are asked"*. So, are you asking?

THE FIRST STEP...
~ ASK your Angel, reach out to them with your wants; your desires; your needs. Ask your

Angel for this to be for your Greatest and Highest good; or better. Your personal Angel knows what you need, but cannot just assume that is what you want. The Angels will give you precisely what you are asking for; so be specific!

THE SECOND STEP...
~ TRUST that your Angelic help is on its way. All Angels must abide by the Universal law stated above, so rest assured that one of them will help you. They will open doors for you and guide you in the right direction. If you are not trusting in them, you will miss the help they are sending to you.

THE THIRD STEP...
~ BELIEVE that you deserve to have this guidance from the Angels. Believe, for the Angels 'will' help you when you wholeheartedly believe in them. Believing that you deserve to have what you are asking for is not just asking, its feeling this with your heart.

THE FOURTH STEP
~ THANK YOU – It is very important that you always show Gratitude to the Angels for all that you are about to receive, and all that you 'do' receive; even if it's not exactly as you planned.

Remember, they know us better than we know ourselves, and they know what is for our Greatest and Highest good. With an "Attitude of Gratitude", anything if possible!

Now watch how your life begins to unfold and will continue to unfold as you break down the walls that surround you. As you begin to trust, the help of these Celestial Beings of Light will engulf you in JOY!

In this book; you will learn how to work with Angels; call to your personal Guardian Angel, and learn the aspects with which to help guide you towards a brighter future of healing and love, which is unconditional at all times.

# Contents

Journey of Wings ................................................................. 1

Belief in Angels .................................................................. 6

What are Angels? ............................................................... 8

History of Angels in Religion ........................................... 27

The Hierarchy of Angels ................................................... 40

Who Are the Archangels? ................................................. 48

Angels of Healing and Compassion .................................. 64

Angels to Call Upon for Healing ...................................... 88

Karma and Karmic Debt ................................................... 90

7 Steps to Connecting with Your ..................................... 96
   Guardian Angel

Methods That Angels May Use to .................................. 101
   Communicate

Incarnated Angels, Elements, Walk-Ins ......................... 116
   and Star People

How to Live like Earth Angels Do .................................. 128

Numbers and the Angels ................................................. 130

A Box of Angels .............................................................. 135

Angelic Messages to Use Every Day .............................. 136

Angel Drawing Meditation ............................................. 142

About the Author ............................................................ 147

## ~JOURNEY OF WINGS~

I have designed this book to talk about the Celestial Beings of Light, why they exist in our lives, and how they exist in our lives, so that we may learn how to communicate with them, and how to allow them into our lives.

All my life, I have seen wonderful swirling lights in colours, unimaginable to the human mind; often hearing beautiful music surrounding me when I saw them. Then, one day, the quest to have my questions answered ended in a journey which I shall never forget, yet it is one that I will always remember. I return there often.

Towards the end of my illness with cancer, I began a new journey of Spiritual enlightenment which led me to learn the art of Meditation; being still and just one with one's self. One day, my journey brought two incredible Lights of the Highest Order to me who brought me to a castle in the sky known as the *'Crystal Palace'*.

As we approached the grand doorway made of the finest mahogany wood, there upon the door was my 'Soul' name, and immediately, I knew where I was on the loving list of names. I reached out and touched the engraving and it felt 'real', and suddenly, I knew I was home. As my fingers touched the letters, the doors magically began to transform becoming a portal to the other side. These Beings of Light escorted me inside.

Once we entered in the door, there was a grand palace. Stained glass windows adorned the walls which were made entirely of crystal. Off the main room there were smaller rooms, but in the centre was a small cleansing pool with a waterfall of Pure White Light. The Light came from the sky though an opening in the clear crystal ceiling, filling the pool but never overflowing it. My Celestial Lights escorted me to stand in the centre of this pool, where I was showered with this cleansing White Light. It was in this Light that answers were given to me; I was welcomed home. I could now understand what the music meant. Like soft voices in my ears, I understood what they were saying to me, and all my questions could be answered because I could now understand the voices of the Angels.

I understood; these Lights are the Angels of Heaven, and all the existing galaxies in the cosmos. Each Light; each Angel is to God what a ray of sunshine is to the Sun. Showing me, teaching me all I needed to know so that I may share with you. Each day continues to be like a day in the classroom. So much to learn from them, so much that I have learned from them and so much to share. I have become the teacher.

When a Soul is created for the first time it is but a mere ball of Light; perfect Love and perfect Light. This Light is then given to an Angel, and this Angel must watch over the Soul-Light for eternity. When this Soul-Light incarnates into human, it is because it has decided to incarnate, and has received permission from the Creator to come to the Earth. This planet Earth, which holds a greatness of violence, hatred and volatility more than any other planet or star form in any galaxy. This planet Earth, where each living being needs protection. Upon each lifetime that *any* Soul chooses to incarnate, it needs the protection of greater proportions. This is called your *personal Angel*, or your *Guardian Angel*. The keeper of your Soul.

### ARE YOU ASKING?

Many are asking, but we ask in panic, or out of sheer desperation, not understanding that things take time; our time. In this book, you will learn some simple techniques about asking, and more importantly, how to receive the answers directly from your Angels.

Angels don't belong to only one religion, or only to those who pray, or to only those who are good. Angels are for everyone and we all have the right to ask. More importantly, you *'deserve'* to receive. We all deserve to receive.

This book will be your guide to the Angels and will become your own personal connection to them. You will get to know them, to talk with them and to listen to you. Feel them in your heart. Bring them in for complete wholeness. Complete Love.

Open you heart, and your life to these incredible beings of Love and Light. Let them help you to feel the Joy that is your life, even when you don't think there is any. Let them in and allow them to teach you Peace.

Angels have made a tremendous resurgence into the life of people on the planet Earth in the last 30 years. We see more on television, more books being written and more encounters with their Celestial presence. It is never a coincidence when an Angel has made their presence into your life.

Let **your** journey begin with this one small step.

*"Angelic Messages are always Loving, Positive and clear; even though they may be sobering. They do not leave the receiver with feelings of anxiety or unwanted fears, but with feelings of confidence and knowing that within; that the messages are right and true. Truly, Angelic Messages only come from God."*

## ~BELIEF IN ANGELS~

The belief in Angels is a Universal phenomenon. Before you begin working with them you have to decide what constitutes them to be and what doesn't. It is best to leave your mind open, simply because no one person can tell you what they are like, you have to decide what constitutes them to be and what doesn't. Angels are what you perceive them to be.

Here are some questions to '<u>think</u>' about to get in touch with your own personal feelings on Angels:

1. Do you believe **all** Angels look alike?

2. Do you think Angels will appear before you in this dimension, talk to you in your head or just send you ideas or inspiration?

3. Do you think Guardian Angels or Celestial Angels are the same or different?

4. Do you think Ghosts and Angels are the same or different?

5. Do you believe Spirit Guides and Angels are the same or different?

6. Do Angels have to have a name?

7. Do all Angelic names have to end in 'el' or 'irion'?

8.  Do you feel that because an Angel received its name through a religion that's different from yours, you can't work with it?

9.  What do Angels look like?

10. Can humans be Angels, or are Angels a species unto themselves?

I'm sure that you have your own ideas on Angels that are not covered here today, that's Okay! The idea in asking these questions is to get you **'thinking'** about Angels – <u>not</u> to test you on what the right or wrong answers may be.

## ~WHAT ARE ANGELS~

The purpose of this book is to teach you how to get to know your Guardian Angel and the Angelic realm. To help you communicate with your own personal Guardian Angel. Let's begin by talking briefly about the different energies that one may find around them. Energies that lie within the realms that are beyond ours. It is important for us to understand these different energies so as not to confuse a dear loved one with that of an Angelic presence.

What are Angels? A question often asked of me. We all have some idea of what we believe these Celestial Beings to be. During our childhoods, we may have been taught that Angels are winged creatures donning long flowing robes with halos and often carrying flaming swords or staffs. These Celestial Beings are gloriously depicted in books and paintings. Beauty for the eye to behold.

When talking about Angels we must first talk about some of the other existing energies that are around us. Energies that aid us on our journey of life; towards our destination. This does not include Earthbound Angels, or Star people, which we will be discussed later in this book. For they are beings whose existence is on the planet and not between the veils.

There are five categories of Light Beings which find themselves 'between the veils' on this planet. They are: Ghosts, Spirits, Spirit Guardians, Spirit Guides and Angels. Other incarnated energies born into this place and time. I am going to briefly describe to you five energies which may exist around you that you may not see.

Let's begin this journey by talking about one of the most talked about and most misunderstood energies on the planet at present.

**_Ghosts_** - In this time of uncertainty and a time where *'reality TV'* shows have taken over the boxes in our living room which we call *televisions*. More and more of these reality shows are being created to showcase or to exploit Ghosts, the paranormal or the supernatural. Some have a positive impact on our society while others are having a negative impact. Without getting into the technicalities of what these energies are (let's save that for another book), these restless spirit energies are the first stage of death after life; energies of a Spirit-Light that gets stuck between the veils, or levels of consciousness known to man. Our Soul's spirit energy passes through them as we descend to the Earth, and once again as our spirits travel back home after death.

A Spirit-Light can get stuck between the veils as they ascend home for a variety of reasons. They can be holding back for a purpose. They may have a message that needs to be delivered to the living, or they may just not know that they are without a body; dead. There may be many reasons this could happen. The Soul may have unfinished business or attachments to places or things. They could be holding onto anger, or someone could be holding them back because of their grief. In most cases, they need to be shown the Light, and helped to cross over to the next destination of the Soul's journey to be able to continue.

Death is what occurs naturally for the body; the vehicle in which the Soul is transported to on this planet. Death is about transcending into the next life. When our body expires, the Soul sometimes does not realize this and thinks that it is still living. When no one can see or hear them, this confuses them or makes them angry. So the energy of the Soul becomes a ghost, and will seek out guidance from the living, usually a Medium, who can help them to communicate their message, or help them cross into the Light.

***Spirits*** - When this phantom energy of a ghost has crossed through into the Light; the first veil, they become what is known as a *'Spirit'*. A vessel of Spirit-Light energy that can now cross between the veils, back and forth between the worlds, to contact their loved ones. They can travel throughout the Earth, but not on the Earth without a solid body. They are no longer grounded to the Earth by gravity. Travelling through the veils, they come into contact with the living and they can watch, guide and protect those that were left behind after they died. This allows them to aid those they feel they have left behind. Allowing their Soul-Spirit to go to Heaven, or travel to other people and places. There is really no concept of time for these Souls. Time simply does not exist; it only exists for us on the planet.

**Spirit Guardians** - Often confused with a Guardian Angel; they are not. So then, what are these Spirit Guardians? Spirit Guardians are the Souls/energies of a loved one who has passed, crossed through the veils. This Spirit has the choice to stay for a while, or to cross back to incarnate once more. This is a choice each Soul-Spirit has; to become a Guardian; to watch over someone who was special to them in their lifetime they last lived in. In this state of 'Spirit', the Guardian is better able to assist their loved one. Sometimes more than they could when they were alive.

It has been through my own personal experience that I come to share this information with you. It was after the passing of my mother, when I personally came to experience this first hand, how this phenomenon actually works. To talk to my mother and understand that she is watching dutifully over my daughter, and why. When she first passed, I prayed for her and I felt her presence all around. When I bought my first house shortly after her passing, all the signs that I had asked for began to present themselves to me. All that she had her hand in seemingly fell into place. She made certain to let us know it was her presence that allowed this to happen and she still makes her presence known to us. Even now, she gives us a spirited knowing that she is indeed with us. It could be through the waft of her cologne or through the dimes that fall out of nowhere, or when we have asked for her guidance. (Yes, you can ask for guidance and help with your journey.)

***Spirit Guides*** - In the many years of my working with people, I have had visits with many different energies and spirits which have come forth to speak to me. Though it is through my own personal experiences that I have come to understand the true meaning and purpose of Spirit Guides. Spirit Guides, or Guides, come through and make their presence known to me during readings and healings with clients so that I can relay their messages and for what purpose they have come through.

I see these Guides come and I hear them speak. When I ask them individually, who they are or where they are from, they reveal that they are from the past life experiences of our own lives.

Spirit Guides are Souls that have 'evolved' spiritually, and like the Spirit Guardian, they have chosen to come to be with a specific Soul. This can happen for many reasons. It could be a lesson on their journey that needs to be completed, or for a debt that needs to be repaid. It can be any of these reasons. They have also shown themselves to be in one's life as a Guide to help one move forward on one's life journey; bringing with them guidance and opening doors.

**_Angels_** - A higher evolved energy, and the purpose for this book, but we needed to talk about the other four energies so that we can understand how different Angels are from the other energies that are around to help us through this journey. Angels are a frequency of light above any other living being, past of present that exist within the physical realm. Even higher than that of an Incarnate, Star-person or Walk-In. In order for them to take on a physical form, they are given 'ego', which slows down the frequency level of these Beings of Light so that they may interact and communicate with the living.

Angelic energy is warm and its beautiful; it is comforting and above all, it is gentle. Angels are beings of Pure Love and Pure Light. When encountering one, at first you may feel overwhelmed by the loving energy, but you will never feel fear when an Angel is near. Embrace the heavenly feelings that your Angel will bring to you. Angelic Love is *unconditional*. They open your heart for you to find the True Love that lies within yourself and within your heart. Love for yourself; Love for others.

Each of us resides within our own personal Guardian Angel. We are given one Angel who is our Angel of birth and our Angel of death. One personal Angel who is with us through *each* lifetime. Each life is a life that our Soul chooses to incarnate into. It is this personal Guardian Angel which helps you to transcend, and to break the chains of Karma so we can all evolve together in peace and in harmony. Their energy is soft and gentle, extremely peaceful, yet so very powerful; showing us that the power of Love is the strongest power there is.

Angelic vibration is a very high vibration, or frequency, and time does not exist for these Angelic vibrations of Light. Angels travel to the past, present and future in the blink of an eye. They are everywhere; anywhere, yet nowhere, in the world, all at the same time. They do not live within our time-space continuum, for they are *Omnipresent*; always present everywhere.

There are telltale signs that will show you when an Angel has passed by or when an Angel is near. You will always know when they are near because of the sense of blissful Love overwhelming you, but the feeling will always be a positive loving one. You may see a 'flash' of light, or hear an Angelic tone; a high pitched, soft beautiful song as they sing to you. The Angels sing a song of Peace and of Love; a beautiful song. If you ever see a white feather it is a sign they are near. Angels will always let you know they are near. So pay attention to the signs in your life.

Your intentions come from your Core Star; which is a level that is deep within you. It is this very essence in your core that is beyond emotions; beyond mental and physical body thoughts. Your intentions are powerful as they create your life experiences. Whether it is your intention to choose to make something happen or not, your thoughts are powerful.

Make sure your actions, thoughts and feelings reflect the true intentions which you desire and need to succeed on your life path. Make sure your intentions are Divine and honourable.

The Angels ask that you *'choose'*, and *'infuse'* your thoughts with Love. See yourself and those around you as happy, successful and content. Angels can help you replace negative mental habits with more loving and empowering thoughts. Just ask for their assistance. Call to the Angels of Love and of Light and ask them to fill the whole of your existence on every dimension, and they will. Angels of cleansing and purification will also lend a hand in helping you to achieve these goals, you only need to ask.

Every person, place or thing has a distinct Light energy; a vibration/frequency connected to it. So, by asking the Angels to help you, they will work quickly to help. In accordance to the Divine Plan, they will do what is within their means and power to help and to guide you, without infringing on your *Free Will*; something that is not allowed. Angels love you unconditionally so when you call upon them, you will feel their warmth and Love. You will feel their gentle energy surrounding you. They listen to everything you say, think, and feel. Release all your stress and worries to them and they will, in return, transmute all these negative energies into Love and Light.

Angels will gently guide you to your dreams, and throughout your everyday life. However, Angels will not do all the work for you. They will gently guide you and will show you new energies. They will offer you the opportunities to walk through the doors they have opened which may lead you to where you would like to be/go in your life. Just know that they are there and they will always be there, even when you feel they are not. At times it is important for you that they stand back, so that you can find your own way. Even if that is only way to ask for the guidance you seek.

Guidance will come to you in all forms of synchronicities, and *'coincidences'*. Follow these signs for they are signs that are directing you and confirming to you that the Angels are on your path, where all your dreams will come true. It is important to recognize that there is no such thing as a *'coincidence'*, for a coincidence is your Angel stepping in.

Angels are amazing in that they work on a very high vibration and their limitations are none. Limitations to the Celestial Beings simply do not exist. The Angels and Archangels (discussed later) have a very powerful effect on your life when you work with them.

> **Open your heart to everything around you, everything inside you & let" your light shine forth."**
> ~*Radzekiel*~

In the modern world, Angels are making vast appearances, and to some it is for the first time. Are they *'re-awakening'*, or have they always been around us? Are we just now taking time to listen to the messages they have for us? These are messages of Hope and of Love and of our true destiny. Is this 'new'? Why then are we just taking notice of these Angelic Beings? What is happening in this modern world that we are opening our conscious minds to other worlds and realms?

This tremendous resurgence of interest in Angels has become such a Universal phenomenon that is continuing to remain a persistent force in the human consciousness. It has become clear that something deeper is truly going on. There is a great urgency in these troubled times to understand the collective spirit within ourselves. Angelic communication is just the beginning of looking deeper within our own Souls and listening to what lies within it.

Our present devotion is but the latest in a long tradition that has sought many to preserve this sacred mystery. This mystery should not be preserved. The answers to our true destiny lies within us if only we reach out to the spiritual teachers, the listeners, and the guidance which exists, all at the fingertips of our Soul.

So, what is an Angel? Simply put, an Angel is a direct link to the Creator; as a ray of sunshine is to the Sun. *"Angels reveal our true path to God"*.

Angels are Celestial Beings of Pure Love and Pure Light. They are, in their truest from, being without bodies. They possess superior intelligence, gigantic strength and surpassing holiness. Simply put, an Angel is a *'messenger of God'*. But are the Angels 'simple'?

Angels, are portrayed in some of the great Masters' artwork in a human form, with long flowing gowns, surrounded by bright white lights, halos above their heads, and large swan like wings; gossamer wings.

So, why are they portrayed this way? Angels have a great sense of decency and discretion. They will appear in a form that is kind and gentle. They will show themselves in ways that humans can understand, they can appear as human Angels, touching your life briefly and then they are gone. An Angel will never frighten you, for if we begin to fear them, we will not call upon them. In the North American Native culture, Angels will reveal themselves in animal form. Why? Because the Native people revere the animal kingdom as sacred and blessed.

An Angel may *never* appear as a loved who has passed. This can be too discerning and can upset the human consciousness. This form of energy is of a different nature, as we spoke about in the beginning of this chapter.

So, then, where DO these incredible creatures truly come from? Why are they here? Let this journey begin as we unravel the basic understanding of these truly incredible Beings of Light.

**Let me start at the Beginning**: If you are going to tell a story; a story which is part of an even greater story, what better place to start than at the beginning. So, let us go back, back to a time before time began, time as we know it.

Life begins with the creation of a Soul; a being of Light and energy, also known as your 'Soul-being'. These crystal lights, as created by the Creator, were created solely *for* the Angels, to give them an understanding; that clearly became their purpose, which is to care and watch over this spectacular life form. **You truly ARE!** So, in making sure that nothing ever would happen to this perfect creation of 'God'; a.k.a., your Soul, this Light Being has come to be in the custody of an Angel to protect and watch over this new Light source.

Then the Soul began to feel restless, and that is when something wonderful began to happen. The Soul was given permission from the Creator to come to Earth; given a body for transportation and a new path with a purpose; a purpose as chosen by the Soul to give sustenance as to why they are on the planet. Each Soul has an intertwining path that is connected to one another, each having six degrees of separation amongst them. They are also gifted with an ego; yes gifted. This is so the Light of the Soul does not lose its way, so it will remain grounded on this, the most volatile and violent planet there is in this Galaxy. Of course, not to be left out, the greatest gift of all that is given is, of course, **Free Will**! The freedom to make decisions and choose lessons as you go about your life.

So then, what happens to this 'all-encompassing' being of Light called an 'Angel', that is to be our Guardian against all the evils of the Earthly planet? What becomes of these Light Beings when we are given these things?

These Beings of perfect Love and of perfect Light, these extensions of Creator, must now abide by a Universal Law given to them which states: *"No Angel shall interfere with a human's life unless there is a life threatening emergency or, unless they are asked."*

Angels want to surround us, they want to make our life pleasant and untroubled. It is their greatest Joy to take away all of your hurts, fears and stresses. 'Our' Joy is their greatest pleasure. Yet they cannot intervene in this task, unless we *'ask'*. An Angel will not make decisions for the human, but when asked, it is their Divine pleasure. They may offer advice and different ways to view the situation. They open doors for you to pass, but they may never do the work for you. Later, we will discuss the many ways of communicating with your Angel.

So, an Angel may nudge you, they will encourage you and may even create miraculous 'coincidences' for you … but they cannot help unless you have made the conscious choice to accept and receive; because you have, "*free will*". It is one of our greatest pleasures to receive all that the Angel can give to us, but we must be willing to open up to them, as they are open to us.

# ~HISTORY OF ANGELS IN RELIGION~

There is much that has been written on the history of the Angels. In each bible and in each religion there has been some experience with these beings of Celestial Light we call Angels. In this chapter I will talk only briefly of how Angels have impacted humanity.

Angels do not belong to Religion, but they belong to each of us. Or rather, we belong to them. It is your right to have your personal connection to them.

With this tremendous resurgence of this life force on our planet, it is important for us to take a journey into history to see how the Angels appear, and how they have evolved in our hearts over the centuries.

**Where Do We Begin?**

The word Angel, in Greek, means messenger. For thousands of years, evidence of the Angels has been believed to have existed in many religions and cultures. People talk about them and believe in them. Long before man had ever entered their presence onto the Earth. They are the guardians of life to all living things; to all life, life everlasting. So how did our recollection come to be?

The first known existence of Angels emerged around 1000 BC with the Persian religion, Zoroastrianism. In Judaism the concept of Angels stems from the influence of Persian culture.

The earliest known writings of Angels are found to be in the Dead Sea Scrolls. Writings can also be found in the book of Enoch and the book of Talmud and Zohar. All of these writings relate God, Angels and humans.

> *"The meaning of Angels is the confirmation of God and his Celestial power. These are of the kingdom heavenly; these are of God Spiritual."*
> ~Baha'I~

Written in the Dead Sea Scrolls, in the scroll called 'the Copper Scroll' is a list of the material possessions of the 'Essences'. The Essences at the time were known within their community to be quiet and gentle and were very strict within their beliefs that the physical body is a temple of the Soul. These Essences were attuned to the Angels as a daily part of their everyday existence. So they developed a tree of life that represented fourteen Angelic forces.

Angels do not belong to religion, not even one religion, but throughout time they have appeared in scripture and in the artwork in Cathedrals. The Bible says that God appointed Angels to those who love God and call to Him.

*"For He shall give His Angels charge over you, To keep you in all your ways."*
Psalms 91:11

The Bible refers to different types of Angels, with varying duties such as guides, protectors, messengers and Angels of the Lord. In the sixth century, Dionysus the Areopagite, a monk, wrote a treaty depicting three spheres of the Angelic Hierarchy. The First Sphere are the Seraphim, Cherubim and Thrones. The second consist of the Dominions, Virtues and Powers. And the third, the closest to humans, are known as the Principalities, Archangels, and Guardians, or 'Angels'.

*"They are not to be worshipped for they are creatures."*
Col. 2:18; Rev. 19:10; 22:9

Angels, their meaning, their appearance and their purpose has varied throughout history and throughout the world in many forms. Many artists have given us their visions of Angels as winged creatures, usually beautiful figures with gossamer wings draped in cloth that glow; shining and floating in human form or as a voice. Saints, and even everyday people, in history have told stories about being visited by and/or helped by Angels.

In the Bible, Angels have appeared as messengers, guides, and healers.

> *"And I beheld and I heard the voice of many Angels round about the throne, and the number of them was thousands of thousands."*
> ~ St. John, the Evangelist~

Angels are even recorded in the Koran.

> *"You shall see the Angels circling around the throne, giving glory to their Lord".*
> ~Koran~

Throughout the world there is great literature and art that tell us of the many tales of Angels. Yet, the common thread that weaves amongst these legends and the lore is the undeniable influence that Angels have had upon nearly every culture and religion known to man.

Hebrew concepts formed the background for Christian beliefs concerning Heaven and Angels. Some scholars say that the earliest religious representation of Angels was found at Ore, the Sumerian capital of the Hebrews. A winged figure is shown descending from Heaven to pour water from an overflowing jar into the cup held by a king. Others suggest the earliest depiction of Angels is found in the annunciation scene at the catacombs of Priscilla in Rome dating from the 2$^{nd}$ Century AD. But archaeological remains of the earliest Christian church found in Syria that was built or remodeled in 233 AD do not show any pictures of Angels. A synagogue found in the same spot however shows robed figures attending Moses. For the early Christian church, the time of the Angels had not yet come. It wasn't until the reign of Constantine the Great from 306 to 337 AD that Christian art began to flourish and then we began to see the characteristic appearance of Angels.

*"Behold, I send an Angel before thee, to keep thee in the way, and to bring thee into the place which I have prepared. 21 Beware of him, and obey his voice, provoke him not; for he will not pardon your transgressions: for my name is in him. 22 But if thou shalt indeed obey his voice, and do all that I speak; then I will be an enemy unto thine enemies, and an adversary unto thine."*
~ Exodus 23:20~

> *"Through the Angel who appeared to him in the burning bush, Moses was sent to be their ruler and savior."*
> ~Adversaries. Acts 7:35

Some people entrust their lives to Guardian Angels, or believe when they die they will be led to Heaven by the Angel of Death. There are claimed to be warrior Angels who lead us into battle. Some churches and museums are decorated with the images of Archangels, Seraphim and Cherubim. The great religions have tried to define the Angels and give them names, while theologians and philosophers have argued their nature and meaning.

> *"For the Lord Himself shall descend from Heaven with a shout, with the voice of the Archangel, and with the trumpet of God: and the dead in Christ shall rise."*
> First: 1 Thessalonians 4:16,17 / KJV.

Throughout the Scriptures there are warnings about dreams, visions and false prophets. The Apostle Paul wrote,

> *"Let no one keep defrauding you of your prize by delighting in self-abasement and the worship of the Angels, taking his stand on visions he has seen, inflated without cause by his fleshly mind..."*
> Col. 2:18

> *"For the Son of Man will come in the glory of His Father with His Angels, and then He will reward each according to his works."*
>
> Matt. 16:27

In history, world cultures and religions, Angels have been thought of as creations of a separate order from human beings and also as the spirits of highly evolved humans. Angel scholar, Geddes McGregor, tells us the English word 'Angel' is a transcription of the Greek word "agaylos". In Hebrew, Angels are called "mal'ak", meaning messenger. "Mal'ak" originally meant shadow side of God. The Hebrews thought of Angels as emanations of Yahweh, part of the same Divine Spirit. In the Christian church, Angels were not believed to be emanations of God, but spirits created by God at the time He created the material world. Muhammad said Angels were sent by God to seek out those places where men and women honour the Deity. The Angels then report back to Heaven what they have heard. Angels have been thought of as creations of a separate order from human beings and also as the spirits of highly evolved humans.

Socrates tells us that Eros is a spirit who carries messages back and forth between men and gods. Another Angel-like figure from mythology is Hermes, the winged messenger. Nike, or Victory, with her great wings served as a model for later depictions of Angels according to art scholar Peter Lamborn Wilson. We also find similar beliefs in supernatural beings in the vision of the Shaman. The Shaman takes a bird form, travels in search of the Soul of his patient. Primitive cultures generally thought that illness was caused by loss of Soul of some kind. There have always been people employed to go and find the Soul, whether its contemporary psychologists or ancient healers.

In the middle ages, St. Augustine described the nature of an Angel by relating it to an Angel's purpose.

*"The Angels are spirits, but it is not because they are spirits that they are Angels. They become Angels when they are sent. The name Angel refers to their office not to their nature. You ask the name of this nature, it is spirit. You ask its office, it is that of Angel. In as far as he exists, an Angel is a spirit, and as far as he acts he is an Angel."*

~St. Augustine~

## ANGELS AND THE KABALA:

*"In the beginning God created the Heaven and the Earth. And the Earth was without form and void; and darkness was upon the face of the deep. And the Spirit of God moved upon the face of the waters. And God said, "Let there be light": and there was light. And God saw the light, that it was good: and God divided the light from the darkness?"*

Genesis 1:1-5

**The Kabala** is a body of information; one of the richest sources of Angelic lore that was written in early Jerusalem. The word 'kabala' in Hebrew comes to mean *'to receive inner wisdom by word of mouth'*. This original wisdom was an oral one which was passed from master to student.

**Origins** was originally written as the book of Zohar or the book of Splendour. This is known as the credited works of Melchizedek, priest-king of Salem, Jerusalem. It is believed that this book of Zohar was passed to the father of the Jewish nation, Abraham.

The Kabala has been used by many for centuries by Mystics as a map to experience various aspects of creation. Mystics believed that this book was their route back to God.

The existence of the Kabala shows different stages through which God brought the Divine scheme of life into manifestation… **the Tree of Life**.

Mystics who studied the Kabala regarded this book as their manifestation of a core reality reinforcing the elements that represent a structure of existence. Divine energy descends from above and gives rise to ten *'Sephiroth'*; vessels, spheres, points of light. Each Sephiroth represents a power. An energy which is a seen as a signature on the tree must then balance each other. *"As above, So below"*.

This *'Tree of Life'* can be viewed upwards to God-consciousness, by ascending from the base of the tree to the top of the tree in reverse order; although a more direct route is available through the center source of the tree. This can be used as a guide with whatever your belief system may be. Thus you will be able to comprehend the several processes by which you may access the Divine energy into your own life, and arrange your life in accordance to your own life perceptions.

Here are the basic principles. There are 10 Sephiroth, each one has an interlocking path; 22 interlocking paths giving you a total of 32 paths of wisdom in total. Lying between each of these 32 paths are 50 gates of Light that make up the *'Tree of Life'*.

Each of these 10 Sephiroth was assigned a letter of the Hebrew alphabet and named according to its function; each has an associated Archangel working with it, holding its energy pattern. The Hebrew alphabet consists solely of consonants, and each is believed to hold a sacred vibration of sound. It is believed that in this sound holds its own unique creative cosmic-power. A power that is only activated by the human voice.

Kabbalists believe that when prayer is spoken loudly it activates this cosmic power of God through the consonants spoken; opening each of these paths. Channeling down through the Tree of Life and into your vehicle body; permitting the will of God. With the gift of your collective *'free will'*, you can use the Kabala with its 32 paths of this wisdom, as a source in which to fully integrate and utilize the attributes of the Sephiroth in your daily life.

You can work with the Angelic realms by committing to learning, and working towards a greater self-knowledge, and wisdom of the Angels and the basic principles of the Kabala. When the Archangels channel the energies of the Creator, they are like generals commanding their troops to draw down these energies to each of the lower spheres. Each Archangel also has a special place in the web of Creation which they hold, and each is assigned a specific frequency enabling it to act as an archway into each of the Spheres with different energy vibrations.

# ~THE HIERARCHY OF ANGELS~

### *The Angelic Hierarchy; beginning from Heaven to Earth.*

In order to closely connect with the Angels, it is important to understand this Hierarchy of the Angels if you are going to understand and work with Angels. And to know that each of the Angels governs according to each Sphere in which it resides in. Understanding that this will help you know which Angels to call upon for the help you need.

## The 9 Choirs Of Angels

In the Sixth Century; Dionysus the Areopagite, was commissioned to write a treaty depicting the three Spheres of the Angelic Hierarchy; beginning from Heaven to Earth.

In order to closely connect with the Angels, it is important to understand this Hierarchy of the Angels, to know that each of the Angels governs according to each Sphere. This will help you to know which Angels to call upon for the task at hand when you need their help.

Each of these three Spheres of the Hierarchy is then further broken down into three Choirs of Angels. Each Sphere, and each Choir within that Sphere, is designated to a specific aspect of the Universe. Each aspect enable the 'ebb and flow' of energy to be consistent running between Heaven and Earth; transmuting the energy to and from wherever it is needed; filling the pockets, and gaps where there is no energy. In order for life to exist as we know it, there must be this ebb and flow between Heaven and Earth.

The Angels that are depicted in the First Sphere are known as the '*Angels of the First Sphere*'. They are closest to the 'I AM' presence, the Creator, and are known as the Order of the *Seraphim*, the *Cherubim* and the *Throne*

## Angels of the First Sphere

**Seraphim -** The word means '*to Adore*'; these highly evolved beings are the closest to Divinity and are considered to be the highest order of the Angelic realm; closest to God (*I AM*). In Jewish faith, the *Seraphims* are said to *"sing the I AM's praise"*. *Kodoish, Kodoish, Kodoish*. They concentrate on the vibrational manifestations to keep Divinity intact and constant. Balancing the movement of the planets, stars, and the Heavens using sound and encircling Divinity to ensure its continued existence and they funnel energies towards us so that we keep going. The *Seraphims* balance the movement of the planets, stars and the Heavens using sound. The 'fiery spirits'; usually pictured with six wings and flames. This order is led by Uriel.

**Cherubim** - *"Those who intercede"*. These are the Guardians of light and stars; creating and channeling positive energy from Divinity, and appearing in exquisite form. Their name: *Cherubim* means 'wisdom'. They are not the cute little child-like *cherubs* we see as child-like Angels. In fact, *Cherubims* are known to be the record keepers of Heaven and are often depicted on the Ark of the Covenant as Guardians and record keepers of Heaven. The *Cherubim* watch over the galaxies collecting and dispersing energies whenever and wherever needed. They are often seen or depicted in pictures as Angels with multi-eyed peacock feathers to symbolize their *'all knowing'* characters. They know and contemplate the "I AM" (God) presence. This second order is led by Jophial.

**Thrones** – The Guardians of the Universe. Each *Throne* has their own planet to govern. The 'Earth' *Throne* is the Guardian over our planet. Archangel Michael is the *Throne* now appointed to preside over Earth. The *Thrones* are good to work with when healing the planet(s). These are the 'many-eyed' ones are represented as wheels of fire to Divine Majesty. Led by Japhkiel, they receive directly from the "I AM's" Divine perfection and awareness. *Thrones* take great interest in human activities and they will channel energies from the Divine to your Guardian.

### *Angels of the Second Sphere*

***Dominions*** - It is said that these are the Angels that hold a golden staff in one hand and the "I AM's" (God's) seal in the other. They carry sceptres and swords to symbolize Divine power over all Creation; led by Zadkiel who regulates the duty of Angels.

***Powers*** - These are the Angels in charge of Birth and Death. They belong to this lineage as they keep track of human history, and they organize all the world's religions, by sending Divine energy to keep the positive aspects of them going. The Powers are believed to be the Peacekeepers of the Akashic records (these are the records that hold all thoughts and actions occurring during each Soul's evolutionary journey). They are great protectors and they protect us from evil.

***Virtues*** - The 'shining ones'. They radiate shining light and transmit enormous beams of the Divine Light. They are considered to be the Angels of miracles and of Ascension. The two Angels present at the Ascension of Jesus were Virtues.

## *Angels of the Third Sphere*

***Principalities*** - Represented as the protectors of princes and the leaders of people; overseers of large groups and organizations. *Principalities* are the Angels of cities, nations and rulers. If you want to bring in good energies to the government to help promote world peace, these are the Angels you want to work with. They also would like us to work together, as group consciousness is more powerful than individual consciousness. The Angel leading the *Principalities* is Chamuel.

***Archangels*** - The *Archangels* carry the 'I AM's' message to humans and command the 'I AM's' armies of Angels in the constant battle with the 'Sons of Darkness'. Archangels are known as the 'odd bunch', as they come from <u>any</u> of the nine Choirs of Angels. *Archangels* guide your Soul to harmony and wholeness. They are gallantly led by Michael.

***Guardians*** - OUR Angels; our personal guides and our personal Guardians that help us on our life's journey. Celestial Beings closest to humans, they are the intermediaries between the 'I AM' and mortals. We all have one Guardian Angel watching over us. This is the one Angel that we may call on throughout our lifetime. Throughout each lifetime we journey through. They are there as we need their Love, Light and guidance. THEY are our Angels of Life and of Death; our Soul's protector. Some call them our 'higher selves'. No matter what you call them, they are around us to help us feel the Love in our hearts, and the Joy that lives within us.

## *Remember*

* None of these Angels are better than the others

* Your Guardian Angel may come from any of the other nine Choirs

* Keep your mind and heart pure

* Ask for the BEST possible solution for everyone involved

* When problems involve other humans, things may go slow or not as expected – we all have 'FREE WILL' and Divine Timing is crucial

* Don't think that just because you have asked for help from an Angel that you won't have to do your part by tying up any loose ends or do your share in finding a solution

* You may NOT ask an Angel for the help of another Soul, they have *'free will'* ~ you may, however, ask an Angel to 'be with' another Soul

\* ALWAYS, ask to be treated in a fair and thoughtful manner

*ALL Laws; Cosmic and Human are governed by the Angels – they can change your fate, or anyone's fate at any time. But, they will <u>NEVER</u> be a co-conspirator to anything Evil…*

**\*\****All Angels, attune to, and follow the dictates of the Blessed Mother & the Blessed Father*****\*\***

<u>And</u>… when working with the Angels, our only Achilles heel is **"Fear & Doubt".**

## ~ *WHO ARE THE ARCHANGELS?* ~

As we have seen in the last segment, the Archangels are known as the 'odd bunch', coming from any of the nine Choirs of Angels; for they are known to be the only Angels of their Hierarchy to want to work on the Earthly plane. I have been told that there are roughly 144,000 Archangels and they are most commonly known for their work here on Earth.

At some point in our lives, we have gotten to know, or become familiar with the four Archangels. I call them the 'fearsome foursome'. They are *Michael, Raphael, Uriel* and *Gabriel.* These four are commonly found in all of the religious sects. Then there is the group commonly known to me as the 'Super-Seven'. Added to the original four are *Chamuel, Zadkiel* and *Jophial.* Currently, I am working with twenty-four Archangels in my life, who have all been called forth to work with me. But for the purpose of this book, I will keep it simple. You will learn about those which I have aforementioned, as well as *Lord Metatron*. One cannot write a book on Angels without including *Metatron*. Now, I share these familiars with you as they have requested your presence. You will be able to call to them for guidance each and every day. They will come to you.

Where to start... For some it makes sense to maybe introduce them alphabetically, or perhaps in accordance to importance, or rank? No, that won't work because each Angel is just as important as the other, and each Angel has a job that is just as significant as all the others. So, I have allowed this chapter to be guided by the Archangels themselves. I am going to allow them to come through and speak to you.

**Let us begin on our journey to knowing the Archangels...**

**Archangel Metatron:** *(met-a-tron)* - Sitting at the right hand of God, he is seen as the Prince of Angels. The largest of all the Angels I have seen. He stands so tall and so mighty, but don't let his size fool you. He is, by far, one of the Angels most sought after and called upon in this day and age. If seen in all his glory, *Metatron* has a wing span that wraps around the Earth nine and a half times and his layers of feathers on his wings are 72,000 deep. He is often known, and referred to as, the *'many-eyed one'* and the keeper of Peace and Divinity. *Metatron* is the Angel of Ascension with a Light that is so luminous you will see your path home through him. The ultimate goal for all humans; the place where all religions known to man come together; Ascension. He brings with him, when you call to Him, unprecedented Spiritual growth.

*"Dear one, your path to 'home' is on the stillness of your heart. I will guide you through the initiation process and lead you to ultimate healing and ascension. I will aid you through spiritual evolution and enlightenment. Come to me through the light body and I will guide you to the higher states of awareness and eternal bliss."*
~Metatron~

**TO BRING METATRON INTO YOUR LIFE**: Sit in a quiet place, and focus your breathing on your Crown Chakra. If you have one, hold a Herkimer Diamond in the palm of your left hand. This is the stone of the Crown Chakra. See in your mind's eye an illuminous clear light of energy flowing down from above; cascading all over your body. Breathe in this light, allowing this energy of God's mightiest Angel into your higher Chakra; bringing you closer to *Metatron*. BE in this silence for a few moments. Pay attention to your body's sensations. You may feel tingling, and/or a slight pain, like a head-ache. In time, this feeling will go away, and with practice, you will soon not feel any pain at all. Allow yourself to BE in this moment for as long as you need. Practice as often as you need/want. There are no limitations to doing this exercise.

**Archangel Raziel**: *(raz-eye-elle)* - *Secret of God* - The Archangel of secret mystery, the note taker. This Angel gives Divine messages from Creator to mankind, through the Angels or directly himself. His name means 'Secret of God' because he holds all these secrets of Divine information only giving us glimpses of what is Life and Creation, and what is supposed to be, or can be. *Raziel* is bestowed with knowledge and when you receive his incredible insights, your Crown Chakra will be opened with the flame of your own immortality. With his help, you will see your own immortality and Divinity and literally gaze upon the 'countenance of God'

> *"Dear ones, you are the perfection of Divinity and Love. I will open your heart to the vision and voice of God; I am his voice. Allow me to impart these secret mysteries of the Universe to you through gifts of clairvoyance, prophecy and through revelations. Open up to me and I will reveal to you the secrets of Humankind."*
> ~*Raziel*~

**TO BRING THE ARCHANGEL RAZIEL INTO YOUR LIFE:** Sit in a quiet place, and focus your breathing on your Crown Chakra. Hold a clear Quartz Crystal in the palm of your left hand. You may feel as if you are surrounded by a flame of Light. You will not; should not feel its heat at this time. If you do, it will be a slight sensation. Breathe this flame into your Crown and your Third Eye Chakras, allowing this energy of God's Keeper of the Flame in through your higher Chakra.

*BE* in the silence for a few moments, paying attention to your body's sensations. Any sensations you may feel will disperse in time, and this feeling will go away with practice of doing this exercise and soon you not feel any discomfort at all; only the pleasant vibration of *Raziel* as you allow him to *BE* a part of your Soul. Allow yourself to BE in this moment for as long as you need. Practice as often as you need/want. There are no limitations to doing this exercise.

**Archangel Melchezdiek:** *(mel-keez-di-ak)* - Lord *Melchezdiek* is the King of Peace and Righteousness. By taking human form *Melchezdiek* became the King of Salem (Jerusalem) and formed the 'order of Melchezdiek' to co-ordinate the work of the Christ energy here upon the Earth, via the Merkabah. The way of the Merkabah is the way of allowing, or bringing in profound illumination of the Light body into the heart and mind. Let *Lord Melchezdiek* help you with your spiritual growth; call to him as you journey through the Labyrinth.

> ***"Dear ones, allow me to send down light into your mind, and let it travel into your heart. Allow this light to illuminate your Soul so the only the purest healing and Love may come through. I will bring with me the power of the Merkabah to enforce within you the trueness of your chosen path."***
> *~Melchizedek~*

***TO BRING LORD MELCHEZDIEK INTO YOUR LIFE*:** Sit in a quiet place; focus your breathing on your Third Eye Chakra, located in the center of your brow. If you own one, hold a purple Amethyst Crystal in the palm of your left hand. You may feel as a if there is a sense of pure righteousness about you. Allow this energy of *Lord Melchezdiek* in through your Third Eye Chakra. *BE* in the silence for a few moments. Pay attention to your body's sensations. Any sensations you may feel will disperse in time, this feeling will go away with practice of doing this exercise and soon you not feel any pain at all; only the pleasant vibration of the Angel as you allow him to BE in your Soul. Allow yourself to BE in this moment for as long as you need. Practice as often as you need/want. There are no limitations to doing this exercise.

**Archangel Michael:** (*my-k-elle*) - His colour is that of royal blue, with purple and red flashes of Light. His name is a question; 'who is like God'? (the "I AM" presence). The power of Archangel *Michael* is unlimited. He represents truth, courage and protection. He is the protector and guider of pure Love and Light. *Michael*, and his 'band of Mercy', escorts away all negative energies, when burdened by worries and fears. He will guide and protect you. In 1950, Pope Pius XII declared *Michael* the patron of all police officers.

*"Dear ones, I am the new protector of your planet; the protector of the Earth. I stand with God; the I AM presence together, with my band of Mercy to protect all that is Truth and Love on your Planet Earth, we, collectively, keep the order of chaos to the bare minimums, keeping the ebb and flow clean and clear for all to reach their destinies on your planet. Know that war is as it should be, and all is controlled, please do not worry."*

~Michael~

## TO BRING LORD; ARCHANGEL MICHAEL INTO YOUR LIFE:

Sit in a quiet place; focus your breathing on your Throat Chakra, located in the lower throat area (before the shoulders, in front of the body). If you have one, hold a Blue Lace Agate in the palm of your left hand. You may feel a sense of pure calm come over you; you may feel the need to defend. Allow the pureness of his energy of in through your Throat Chakra. Feel free as you drink in *Michael's* sensibility and righteousness. BE in his silence for a few moments. Pay attention to your body's sensations. Any sensations you may feel will disperse in time. You will find these feelings dissipate and go away with practice of doing this exercise. Soon you will only feel the pleasant vibration of the Angel *Michael* as you allow him to BE in your Soul. Allow yourself to BE in this moment for as long as you need. Practice as often as you need/want. There are no limitations to doing this exercise.

**Archangel Gabriel:** *(Gab-rye-elle)* – whose name means, *"God is my Strength"*. *Gabriel* is known as the Messenger Angel, always helping the human messengers. *Gabriel* has been known throughout history as the Angel to reveal God's messages of our times. The mention of him in scripture was to send God's messages to humans. His most infamous words were that of God's news to Mary of Jesus' pending birth, and when he returned to tell of the King's Birth. *Gabriel* is the only Angel to be seen as both male and female, as all Angels are androgynous. Everyone starting something new can call upon *Gabriel*; he/she breathes life into stale situations. Ask for *Gabriel's* help when feeling 'stuck'.

> *"Dear ones, open your heart and your throat chakras to receive my messages. All messages shall be received through pureness of the Soul, and through pure unconditional Love. Allow the words of loving guidance to come through me so that you may receive direction from the Creator, and live your life's purpose"*
> ~*Gabriel*~

*TO BRING ARCHANGEL GABRIEL INTO YOUR LIFE*: Sit in a quiet place; focus your breathing on your Throat Chakra, the

Chakra of communication. If you have one, hold a Blue Lace Agate in the palm of your left hand. You may feel a sense of pure calm come over you, as you feel the need to speak; hush and allow yourself to *BE* in the pureness and in the silence of *Gabriel's* energy. Breathe in through your Throat Chakra. Pay attention to what your body is saying to you. Any sensations you may feel will disperse in time, this feeling and will go away with practice of doing this exercise. Allow yourself to BE in this moment for as long as you need. Practice as often as you need/want. There are no limitations to doing this exercise.

**Archangel Raphael:** *(raf-eye-elle)* - whose name means, *"one who heals"*. He is also known to be around those who travel extensively. *Raphael's* Light is emerald green for healing, and the colour for the Heart Chakra, the Chakra connected with unconditional Love. He is the Archangel in charge of all healing and healers; a guide to those in the healing arts. *Raphael* also gives us ideas and needed information so that we can rapidly heal others. *Raphael* intervenes during medical crises. *Raphael* guides and protects travelers on their spiritual and physical journey. Call upon *Raphael* to clear your path.

> *"Dear ones, allow me and my healing Angels to send healing to you as you need it. Simply call my name and you shall be healed. I bring with me unconditional*

*Love and healing. Allow me into your life, and light your path to wholeness. Healing is yours, for your Greatest and Highest allowed on your path, for your higher purpose."*

~Blessings Raphael~

***TO BRING ARCHANGEL RAPHAEL INTO YOUR LIFE***: Sit in a quiet place; focus your breathing on your Heart Chakra, located in the centre of your chest, where your physical heart is located. This is where true healing begins. If you have a Blue Soda light Crystal, hold it in the palm of your left hand. You may feel your heart flutter a bit as *Raphael* enters in through your body through the truth of you are in the heart. Allow the energy of *Raphael* in through your Heart Chakra. Drink this healing energy in. *BE* in the silence for a few moments. Pay attention to your body's sensations. Any sensations you may feel will disperse in time, this feeling will go away with practice of doing this exercise. Only allow the pleasant vibration of healing as *Raphael*, as you allow him to *Heal* your Soul. Allow yourself to BE in this moment for as long as you need. Practice as often as you need/want. There are no limitations to doing this exercise.

***Archangel Chamuel:*** *(ch-am-u-elle)* - the Angel of Love and Friendships; this Angel fosters tolerance in the human heart, inspiring within us the realization that to love others we must love ourselves. *Chamuel* helps us to drop judgmental attitudes towards others and develop a more tolerant view of our own shortcomings. *Chamuel* is also very technical and can help you when you have trouble with your computer.

> *"Dear ones, open your heart to allow the purest and finest sensations of Love in. In the name of the "I AM" presence, Love is within you completely, and unconditionally. You are whole, and you are complete as Love enters into your heart and your Soul. It is with this within this Love that you will give pure Love, and attract pure Love; unconditionally."*
> ~*Chamuel*~

**TO BRING CHAMUEL INTO YOUR LIFE**: Sit in a quiet place; focus your breathing on your Heart Chakra, located at the heart; the centre of your body, and the place where you hold Love. If you have one, hold a Rose Quartz Crystal; the stone of the ultimate Self-Love in the palm of your left hand. You may feel a sense of Pure Love come over you as your heart flutters, and skips a beat. Hold onto this feeling, as this is the feeling of Pure Love. Allow *Chamuel's* loving energy in through your heart. *BE* in the silence for a few moments. Pay attention to your body's reactions to this pureness of Love as it enters your heart, and encompasses your whole body and Soul. Any sensations you may feel will disperse in time. Allow yourself to

BE in this moment for as long as you need. Practice as often as you need/want. There are no limitations to doing this exercise, do it as often as you need.

**Archangel Uriel:** *(your-eye-elle)* - whose name means *'Fire of God'*. The Angel of Joy, helping us in times of disasters, rescuing us from our own self-imposed crisis. *Uriel* helps us to establish a calm, centered life. *Uriel's* energy is that of a pale yellow shade, sometimes with flecks of red and gold. *Uriel* brings Divine Light and heals painful memories; transforms regrets or mistakes, so we feel stronger and more loving. Ask *Uriel* to take away any burdens related to the past. He will instantly ease your heart and mind of old, un-forgiveness' held toward yourself and others.

> *"Dear ones, it is through your Joy that I work, allow me to lift your spirits to your highest potential. Allow me to show you Joy, feeling in in your deepest Heart Centre, which is you. All of you. You life is about pure Joy - live in your Joy"*
>
> ~Uriel~

**TO BRING ARCHANGEL URIEL INTO YOUR LIFE:** Sit in a quiet place; focus your breathing on your Solar Plexus Chakra, located below the breastbone, in the stomach area. If you have, hold a Citrine Crystal in the palm of your left hand. You may feel a sense of pure calm come over you. Feel your spine straighten as you feel self-confidence. Allow *Uriel's* energy in through your Solar Plexus Chakra. *BE* in the silence for a few moments. Pay attention to your body's sensations. Any sensations you may feel will disperse in time, and with practice, these feelings will go away and you will only feel the pleasant vibration of the Angel *Uriel* as you allow him to *BE* in your Soul. Allow yourself to BE in this moment for as long as you need. Practice as often as you need/want. There are no limitations to doing this exercise.

## ~ ANGELS OF HEALING & COMPASSION ~

When you are sick, feeling lonely, depressed, or you are lacking energy and are unable to motivate yourself; ask the Angels for their healing and for support. You may also choose to do this when you are preparing for, or recuperating from, an operation.

Imagine your body, mind, emotions and spirit becoming a magnet for Angelic healing and for Angelic communication. To be able to ask the guardians to intervene by sending healing energy whenever needed.

Imagine Angels placing hands, wings, or beams of healing Light energy upon any area of your body that is in need of a healing boost, or simply picture them radiating Light directly to your mind, spirit, or emotions. Do this regularly. Every day, imagine their pure White Light gently surrounding your body; feel its love and warmth. This is your Angel's Love.

You never need to worry about asking for more healing than you may think that you deserve. You deserve all that your Angel has to give you, and that is an endless supply. If you are lying in bed recovering from an illness or an accident, you could do this several times, every day. There are no limitations.

Just remember that the more you ask, the more you will receive.

Talk to your Angels. Be specific about your needs and you will be more open to getting what you want and need much more quickly. For instance, if you ask for more money, you could find a penny, or a dime. If you ask to meet someone, you could find yourself in a store talking with a customer, or an employee, and, well, you've 'met someone'. Being specific lest your Angel know precisely what you need. You may think, well, if they know what I am thinking, they should know what I need and want… this is a perfect example of 'free will'. Your Angel may only give you what you are asking for. So, make your intentions pure, and true, and be sure to be specific.

You could ask them to bring you the healing that would help you evolve spiritually; you could ask them to comfort you during times of grief or to heal the cause of your distress. Ask them to bring you the proper care that you need during your crisis. Ask your Angels for their guidance, they will always show you the way. When you ask, the Angels love to point you towards the best possible solutions for you. All you need to do is say is:

*"Angels, I need _____ - Please guide me in the right direction."*

### EXERCISE: *Sending Angelic Healing*

*Find a quiet, comfortable place to sit and relax. Breathe deeply, and allow your eyes to gently close. Use your imagination to contact the Angels of Healing. Simply think: "Angels of Healing, please come to me". You may not ask for healing for someone who is sick, someone who is lonely or isolated, who is grieving, or for any human need that another person may have. However, you may ask the Angels of Healing and Compassion to be with them when they are ready to receive. Everyone possesses the power of 'free will', and you do not know what is ahead on their path. You may send the Healing Angels to someone who is quite well but who you instinctively feel may need a boost of confidence, joy, or inspiration.*

*Begin by thinking of the person with whom you wish to send Angelic healing. You do not have to know them intimately but it does help to know their name. Focus on all the information you have about them and trust the Angels to make the connection with the right person. If you do know this person well, then take a few moments to think of them, remembering how they look or how it feels to be in their company as well as acknowledging their current situation. Ask the Angels to surround this individual with healing energy and provide them with the love and support required to facilitate a process of spiritual transformation. When the time is right, the person in question will know when to accept this healing.*

*Picture this person surrounded by Angels of Healing. Each Angel has a special gift to bring. Some may cheer and comfort; some may offer protection while others may bathe this individual with golden rays of healing Light. If there is physical illness or disease, imagine the Light creating balance and harmony throughout the body. If there is emotional distress, the Light calms and brightens the emotions and brings a new sense of hope. If this person is recovering from an accident, imagine the Angels using the Light to disperse the fear and shock that may surround them and picture all breaks, sprains, burns or bruises healing rapidly.*

*Detach yourself from any preconceived outcomes. Know in your heart that the Angels will take care of your request when the time is right. When the person accepts what is being sent. When you are engaged in absent healing, it is not possible to receive direct confirmation of effectiveness. The healing may not happen right away, but you can be content in sending healing thoughts; asking for the help of the Angels, and trusting that the person in question will receive the healing or comfort when needed. There is no need to doubt the Angels, trust in them, for they will have the situation under control. The form of this healing is dependent of the person's 'free will' and so will vary and so will the results. All we can do is ask for the Angels to intervene, send our loving thoughts and surrender to the will of the Divine. If there is any practical support to be offered, you will be guided to do so.*

## *HELLO, GUARDIAN ANGEL? IT'S ME...*

Encountering your Guardian Angel will change your life; this is a given. This powerful relationship will add to the depth of all your relationships. It has encouraged people to change their lives; to be guided in the right direction. Encounters with Angels brings people to a deeper understanding of their faith and to be more compassionate and empathetic in their daily lives. It will also bring you to a better understanding of yourself in the process as a spiritual being of Light. Angelic guidance will help you to discover your 'free will', and the direction that you should be taking on your life's path. Therefore, before you can come to a truer understanding of your connection with your Guardian Angel, you must first come to terms with the ideals and expectations which surround them.

Different accounts from different cultures portray Angels in different ways. Some as superhuman beings with powers and abilities that can be called Divine or supernatural. When Angels appear, they are *always* accompanied by amazing waves of Pure Love and power. So powerful are these rays of Light, that some are completely overwhelmed by its force. Angels will almost always appear as beings of Light; aura like. This is what true all-encompassing Love looks like, and although they may sometimes appear in human form, they are often seen with large sweeping, gossamer wings, beautiful faces and graceful bodies, adorned in flowing robes of Light.

White is the color most often attributed to them, although many different colors are mentioned in various historical accounts. Angels will appear to you in a manner which provides you with the most comfort, so as not to frighten you. So, they may appear as someone coming into your life to guide you for a short period of time, or a longer period of time. Know that it is not the quantity of time that they spend with you, but the quality of that time they are with you that matters most. This person will then, most mysteriously, disappear from your life, just as they appeared. These are called 'Earth Angels'. Even if you feel that their coming into your life was not what you expected, Angels are to be there for your greatest and highest good. Sometimes we need to learn the hard way, but our Angels will never let us fall! They are always there to pick us up. Their Love is Unconditional.

As discussed in a previous chapter; there are nine Choirs of Angels, from the top governing brass that work closely with the Universe and closely with God, and the Angels that work closely on the Earth with humans. These are the Angels we now wish to focus our attentions on.

In many traditions these Angels are said to guard, protect, and guide all living things. Although plants, animals, cities, and nations are reported to also have Guardian Angels, they in fact are governed by the Elementals Angels {fae, sprites, gnomes, etc.}. The most important are those assigned to human beings. When I speak of Guardian Angels, I am referring to the Divine spirits who help and protect each of us from the moment of birth until the day we leave this Earth. The one specifically assigned to YOU for this, your journey of life here on this plane; the one assigned to guide and protect you for now and for always.

Guardian Angels, even in ancient texts, are described as Divine beings assigned to each person at birth. They embody the will and true understanding of their charge and their job is to protect and help that person through the dangers and transitions of life. They represent, in essence, each person's direct connection to God. The function of the Guardian Angel is the same today as it has been throughout history.

Angels are of a higher Light energy force than we are and therefore there is a tremendous gap that lies between us. We can bridge this gap through Love and Intention; Love and Joy; Love and Faith. When we come to this planet with our 'free will', we forget that our Guardians are there to help and to protect us. We want to conquer all there is on our own. Your Guardian Angel will make a loving effort to bridge this gap and reveal itself to you, usually at a time of extreme need. You may expand this awareness and bridge this gap between you and your Guardian if you have the Love and the will; you need to trust and to believe.

We have limited senses with which we perceive the world, so you can't normally see the Angels who may surround you. These higher Light energy beings are as real as you, but they are of a higher kind of energy than the mortal soul. This energy is usually beyond your perception. You can see only a small part of the Light spectrum that they portray. You can not, for example, see ultraviolet light, but you know it exists. Anyone who has been around pets knows that people usually feel, smell, and hear only a fraction of what animals can. It is obvious that most pets have a sense of something that far surpasses ours. This merely shows that most of us don't seek to enlarge the scope of our experience, of our senses. We could, however, see and hear more if we wanted to.

Don't think that, just because you cannot see something, does not mean it is not real. Your mind "tunes out" many things around you all the time, but if you really pay attention, you will be amazed by the things you are missing. One of the keys to connecting you with your Angel is to increase your ability to perceive. If you are not listening for something, you won't hear it, but if you concentrate with real focus on your senses, it is remarkable what you will pick up. It is in this way, that you can signal your Angel that you are ready and willing to communicate, showing that you are reaching toward its higher level of perception and awareness. Your Angel is waiting for such a signal.

Angels are the purest beings of Love and Light that vibrate their frequency at an even higher level of consciousness than we could ever imagine. So it makes sense that your Angel can be near you at all times without you sensing its presence in your day-to-day life. You have accepted your limited sense as the norm of your existence, but you can change your expectations so that you can bridge the gap between you and your Angel. Without much effort you will be able to sense and accomplish things that some might otherwise call miracles. With the use of effective visualization techniques, meditations, mental exercises, and prayers, you will be able to see and communicate with your Guardian Angel.

## *Preparing to Communicate With Your Guardian Angel:*

Before you begin to communicate with your Guardian Angel, you must prepare yourself by opening your senses and concentrate on opening your mind. It generally requires both mental and emotional preparation before you are ready to meet and form a lasting relationship with your Angel.

Mental preparation is perhaps the most important task. Before you can deal with something or communicate with it, you have to accept that it exists. Believing is everything.

How many times have you walked past a new picture on the wall or a book out of place on a shelf and not seen it? You missed seeing it because your mind did not expect to see it! If you often lose your keys, sometimes they are right in front of you, but if they are out of place you won't "see" them until someone points them out.

What does this have to do with your Angel? It is important to realize that your Angel is always with you, without you being aware of it. All it takes is one simple shift in your perception to reveal your Divine being to you! It's not that your Angel appears or disappears, they are always there; it is just simply a change in your perception once you believe they are there.

The first step in preparing yourself to meet your Guardian Angel is to change your expectations—change how you feel and how you react and what you think you will experience. When you let go of what you expect, then your experience will come to you just the way that you need it to, and each time you call to them, you will have a different experience. Feel in your heart; believe in your heart, that your Angel truly does exist and you will meet it simply by shifting your perception. When you do, you will be halfway down the path to connecting with your Guardian Angel.

### *MEDITATING ON YOUR GUARDIAN ANGEL:*

*When you perform this meditation for about ten minutes once, or twice a daily, you will feel your vibration changing within you to a higher acceptation of meeting your Angel.*

Find a quiet time of your day. Turn off all phones, and close the door so as not to be disturbed. Sit in a comfortable chair. Allow yourself to be completely relaxed and comfortable. Morning is often the best time for this, when the stresses of the day have not gotten the best of you. If you are not a morning person, then evening is also a good time, before bedtime.

Relax; breathing deeply and rhythmically. In through your nose and out your mouth. Focusing on your breath, releasing your mind, letting your ego leave the room. Focus on your breathing and without attachment, until your mind is quiet. You can sometimes achieve this through a single-minded focus on one specific thought, prayer, mantra or sound to the exclusion of all outside distractions. When your mind is quiet, pray to the Divine in whatever way you wish and find most comfortable. Ask for the removal of any obstacles. Ask for self-knowledge, and/or for greater awareness. Completely and unconditionally.

See a ring of Pure White Light surrounding you and protecting you from any and all harm; filling you with Pure White Light; allowing all stress and negativity to be washed away. Sit and breathe quietly. Breathe this White Light into your body; feeling yourself filled; finding complete peace within you.

Relax and hold this stillness for a couple of minutes. Let the normal distractions and stray thoughts flow out of your mind. Do not seek to stop them, but acknowledge them in your mind, and let them go to be viewed later. Simply hold yourself as still as possible. Let your mind go, but hold to the center of your being; centre of your thoughts. Allow your body to soften; to relax, relax, relax. If in any way you are finding this uncomfortable, stop, and try again at another time. You cannot do yourself harm when you are surrounded by this Divine Light! Relax! And when you are ready, breathe deeply and silently say:

*"Guardian Angel, come to me"*

Exhaling slowly, saying:

*"With Love & Will, it is; so it will be!"*

*Pause,* and repeat the breathing exercise for as long as you like -- in through the nose; out through the mouth. Until you can hold this for five minutes -- then let it fade away. Continue the breathing opening your heart, mind and body to that which is your Guardian Angel. Don't stress over the outcome, if it does not happen after the first time. It will come. No matter what you are seeing or feeling, stay relaxed and stay centered. Do not become emotional or try to force the experience. In this meditation, you are a passive participant and there is nothing for you to be doing; simply accept the experience.

When you have completed this exercise; you will know it as it is. Simply pray (however you feel comfortable in doing so) to the Divine, thanking the Divine Source of Creation for this experience; asking for a growing awareness of the Divine experience and of your Guardian Angel! It is important for you 'let go' of your pre-conceived desires and worldly thoughts during this exercise.

When you are done, see yourself surrounded by White Light and see it disperse and fade into the great Mother Earth. Slowly come back to your physical body, and to the physical world. Record these experiences in your journal! Soon, you will see the changes.

By practicing this simple meditation daily, you will prepare yourself to the connection with your Angel. And you will gain remarkable results in just a week. The effects are cumulative, so persevere!

### *"Dear Angel, Please Help Me…"*

> *"Keep on asking and it will be given to you;*
> *keep on seeking and you will find.…"*
> Matthew 7:7

Angels are the special request agents over the Divine energies of the Earthly plane, and the Universal plane. Special requests can cover many issues, from assistance with tasks, such as finding your misplaced keys, to helping you to helping you to achieve long-term goals. When involving our Angels in our special requests, we are acknowledging the desires of our higher selves. It is fine to ask Angels for help with your goals and aspirations. Although you may think that the Angels should already know what you want and that you shouldn't have to ask, but asking is the positive step that sets actions in motion and will inscribe it in the Divine registry. There is no harm in asking Angels for anything, because they only do things for our greatest and highest good; of all concerned.

With Angel mail, you write your special request on a piece of paper and mail it to the Angels. The written word is said to have a special power of its own. By declaring your wishes on paper and addressing your letter to the Angels you are clarifying your goals and your truest desires. In order for you to make a special request to the Angels, simply write them onto a piece of paper and address it to your own highest Angel. Always be specific in your request, define what you are asking for as clearly as you can. Always add the phrase "for my greatest and highest good; or better". This will ensure that you will get no less than you are deserving to have. Then express your gratitude. Thank the Angels as if the request has already been granted. Angels may sometimes not grant your wish to you as you asked. When asking for your greatest and highest, they may bring you something better.

While teaching a class one time, I had a student who was requesting for her next car to be a Jaguar. She had asked for this to come to her for her greatest and highest, and, she ended up with a BMW. Why? Because the Angels knew things that she was not thinking of. The Angels knew that she could not afford the upkeep or the insurance of the car she was asking for, the Jaguar. So, they brought her what this car meant to her - prestige and class. One more thing to remember, my student ultimately had 'free will', so she could have chosen not to get the BMW and went straight for the Jaguar, but the outcome would not have been for her greatest and highest good.

Any problem in your life cannot be solved at the level in which it was created. If there is someone in your life (boss, spouse, child, co-worker, or a friend) with whom you have miscommunication with, disagreements and arguments over trivial issues, or serious issues, you must first understand that you cannot change the problem, but you can ask to gain a different and new perspective on the situation. Pay attention to what happens the next time you see the person. Look for subtle or obvious changes of heart which you are feeling towards this person and look for what has changed in the areas concerning the disagreement.

## *FIVE STEPS IN SENDING A REQUEST TO AN ANGEL:*

This technique can be used whenever you feel resistance from other people. Write to your Angel, not theirs (free will). Your Angel has access to all of the other Angels, so be sure to state clearly what you want to change within *you* to better understand the person and/or the situation at hand. State clearly what it is you want to understand, and how you want to handle the situation. Clearly specify what it is you would like to do to rectify the situation. You cannot change them, but you do have complete control over *you* and your role in the situation. Is there a lesson you need to be learning?

By using this technique you can help those you care about, helping them to do something positive for themselves. Sometimes, healing comes in the form of helping yourself, or your perspective of any situation. If someone you know needs a healing, release, love or knowledge, write to your highest Angels and ask that they be blessed with what they need the most; understanding to help them through their trying time. This is especially useful to people you know who may have created situations for themselves they can't talk about face-to-face. Maybe the situation involves something that you can or cannot see clearly from the outside and that they are in complete denial about it.

We can experience pain when those we love disappoint us by doing something we don't appreciate or understand. When writing to Angels, with others being the focus of your request, keep in mind that we all have *'free will'*. Expectations about other people will eventually lead you to being disappointed; one way or another. On the other hand, if you don't expect anything and you give and release freely, lovingly and unconditionally, their negative actions will not be allowed to affect you. It is unethical to try to influence someone romantically by writing to that person's Angel, it will not work; it is bad Karma. And even if it does work, it will cause undo heartache and pain. The best thing to do would be to bless them and release them with Love. Angels will in no way co-conspire to do anything *'bad'* or *'evil'*. It is against the laws of Karma and Free Will. Angels are beings of Pure Love and will not succumb to deeds of harm; it is not in their make up for such shenanigans.

If you are meant to be with this person, then they will come to you freely, with no conditions. The Angels want you to be happy, and it's up to you to claim your own happiness first. Then they will guide you to the right person that is meant to be with you on your path at the time.

Spend only three days on writing your request, fold it and seal it; find a special place for it. Out of sight, out of mind. You can keep your requests in a book; others use a box, or their altar. You may even have a special journal especially used for writing these requests to your Angels. After you tuck your request away, be prepared for action. You have asked, now listen intuitively for the messages regarding your request. You may find signs across your path, or you may forget about it until it 'pops' into your mind after it has been answered. Once I wrote my request of 10 things I needed to manifest,. and when I found the list again, all but one thing was granted to me.

**IN SUMMARY:**

1. Define your request. Remember; you will get exactly what you are asking for; so what are you asking for?

2. Write your request on a piece of paper. Specify the Angel you are addressing, for example:

    *"Dear Guardian Angel" or "Dear Angels of Prosperity"; "Dear Angels of Healing" or "Dear Angel of_____."*

    When finishing your request, end it with the phrase **"for the greatest and highest good of all concerned, or better"** or **"for my greatest and highest good, or better".** This is very important because you don't want to infringe on anyone's *'free will'*. Close your request with an expression of gratitude. **"Thank you"** works best when working with Angels. Thank them when you ask for guidance. Thank them again when you receive your guidance. They love to be appreciated just as you love to be appreciated too!

3. Ask that you be released from all that which is blocking you from receiving your Divine gifts.

4. Fold and seal your letter, find a special place for it and that is how you consider it mailed.

5. Wait for a response, the door will open for you; opportunities for action, or feelings, such as peace of mind and knowing that all is well.

And remember to say *"THANK YOU"*

## *ANGELS TO CALL UPON FOR HEALING*

When calling upon the Angels for healing, you can simply call to your own personal Guardian Angel. Some people have brought it to my attention that they would like to have specific Angels to call upon a specific times, or illness in their life or a loved ones. I have compiled a list of some of the Angels I call upon in great times of need for myself and for others. This list is not an "exclusive" list as any and ALL of the Angels are accessible to you.

- *~Asariel:* Insanity, obsessions, delusions, problems that arise from passive-psychism (i.e. panic attacks caused by repression of psychic abilities).
- *~Cassiel:* Arthritis, rheumatism and all dis-ease caused by cold or damp conditions. Works well with diseases of the elderly. She brings lasting relief if not total cure. *Cassiel* is very slow so if there is urgency, invoke her through Archangel *Raphael*.
- *~Gabriel:* Female health issues (including breasts, childbirth, recovery from caesarians). All stomach complaints and recovery from abdominal surgery. Warts, sterility and edema.
- *~Michael:* Any diseases of the heart or spine, including the back and its muscles.

~*Raphael:* General health, all lung and chest complaints. Cancers or other cellular disorders. Particularly benevolent regarding the health of children, birds and small or young animals.

~*Sachiel:* Problems with poor blood circulation, such as varicose veins or piles, and the health of ankles and feet.

~*Chamuel:* All wounds, rashes, infections, measles, chicken pox, an ailment causing eruptions and migraines. *Chamuel* is also known as the patrol of surgery.

~*Uriel:* All problems of the nervous system.

~*Ariel:* Any organic illness.

~*Hayyel:* Animal healing.

~*Chanael:* Heart healing both physical and emotional.

# ~KARMA AND KARMIC DEBT~

Much today is being written about, and talked about where Karma is concerned. Some believe that Karma, or Karmic Debt, is something that we are sent back with in this human experience from past lifetimes, but that is only partly true. The theory that we only bring unresolved issues from past lives, with us into this life, and that we are here to change or correct them is but a fallacy. When Karma or a Karmic Debt is brought with us into each lifetime, from a past, we have chosen to bring it back. When your body leaves each physical lifetime, it becomes a pure form of energy of Love and Light. Our Soul returns to its perfection; perfection as the "I AM" presence created us to be.

As you will read in this Channeled message from *Archangel Metatron*, you will learn about what Karmic Debit is as per the Angel that sits at the right hand of the Creator. Please take this message with you as you will, that which resonates with you.

# KARMIC DEBT

## ~As Channeled by Archangel Metatron~

*"Dear ones, it has become apparent that there is much confusion in your world as to the belief, and to the understanding of 'Karmic Debt'. specially with how you, your Soul, is to clear this in your lifetime. It is with great Love that I come to you at this time, so that I may bring you a greater, deeper understanding of the great illusion of Karma. I have been asked to come to you to explain the discrepancies of what you are reading and what is being said so that you may understand the truth about Karmic Debt, at this crucial time.*

*It is believed by many that you have chosen to bring with you into this lifetime, at this time in the Earth's existence, unfinished business, or things that you believed 'you' need to correct.*

*Let the truth be told to you that, you are a creation of the purest form of Light, the purest form of Love; the essence of a higher frequency than exists on your planet. Creator, who has created you, created you in perfect form, with exceptional Light and Love. It was when you decided to come to the Earthly plane, that you decided to begin another path along the life of your Soul. Your life as you know it now is new. With no repercussions of anything past. No sin that needs to be forgiven.*

*At the time of your re-admittance back into the form from which you have started, you were absolved of all your sins, all of your wrong doings, and even all of your goodness of that lifetime as well. When each of your lives comes to an end, you are returned to the 'Heavens' in perfect form; in perfect Light; in perfect Love. You are perfect. For when you come back through the veil of consciousness, you are forgiven of all sin, absolution and more importantly, cleansed into the purest of forms as you returned home.*

*Each lifetime in which you begin again, starts when you decide what with your path will be. You decide what your lessons will be and how you will learn them. And my lovely, even with whom this lesson will be learned with, and who your teacher will be.*

*So, my dear ones, this 'Karmic Debt' that is talked about upon your planet now is based on each of you cleansing the soul of all that has been created in the lifetime which you are now living.*

*Each life begins, as you take your path towards your chosen role. You come up against choices, and decisions to which you are given free will which will allow you to take up the direction you will soon travel. As you travel upon this your path, towards your destination; your positioning in life becomes apparent. Sometimes you do not like this, and you get frustrated because the path does not take the direction you planned it to go. You question your free will. You doubt that which is already been planned for you, the plan you have hence, chosen.*

*Free will allows you to go forth on your own, living freely, without question, and without doubt. Choosing your direction and your decisions freely. Your Guides and Angels are there to see that no harm shall come to you. Until, you instill a doubt, and you begin to question this path, unbeknownst to you that this is part of your original contract, a contract with the 'I AM' in which you have carefully designed. When it looks as if harm or illness is placed upon your path, you question this direction, as it is to take you in the direction of your chosen assignment of your life. Your final destination. Each challenge you enter into, is exactly as it should be, taking you in the direction of what is to be, lessons to be learned; yours or someone else's.*

*Illness, as chosen by you, reveals many doorways and paths to the truth of your destiny. The truth between you and your Creator. This is the truth which exists only within your own heart. This truth is part of your chosen path. Most of this is chosen based upon the life, or lives, you have created in the past. Believing in some way that you can return to a physical presence and correct your wrongs. Because your Creator, is an all loving being of the Highest form of the Purest Love, the' I AM' allows you to re-create your past, to correct your wrongs. Wrongs, as you believe them to be!*

*One can call 'Karmic Debt' the accumulation of ego based energies that you build up within your heart and being. During the course of one's life, there are a rebound of various effects of all which has been done in one's life as it comes back to you. All thoughts and all actions are sent out to the universe at the time the energy is generated. So if you project a negative or a positive energy into the Universe it will come back to you. In that lifetime, in that moment; at that time. It is not saved up, it is not accumulated creating a great debt that the Creator expects you to re-pay. It is instant, happens in the lifetime in which you are currently living in.*

*It is with great pleasure that I tell you how all Karmic Debt shall be completed within this lifetime. No Karmic Debt has been passed to you from any other lifetime. It is gone and does not exist, for you have completed that lifetime before crossing through the veil of consciousness.*

*So, dear ones, in this lifetime to which you are living right now, in this moment as you are reading my words, you are creating Karma. All that is said and done in this lifetime, shall be repaid you in this same lifetime. Not just as you have put it out into the Universe, but within all the power of the threefold laws. Karma is redeemed to you by the power of three; body, mind, and spirit.*

*All that you think about, dear ones, exist within this threefold law. All that you speak, and all actions acted upon by you are all a part of this Karma. And all shall be repaid to you momentarily in accordance to this threefold law of the Universe.*

*At the end of each lifetime, a wonderful gift is bestowed upon you 72 hours after your Soul has left your physical body, your Soul is enraptured to experience all that you have given to another to feel. So, dear ones, how will you live out the remainder of your life knowing this? Knowing that all the pain you have caused another shall be repented back to you? Will you think before you react? Will you restrain from causing someone else bodily harm, and learn to love more?*

*In accordance to all the Universal, and Spiritual laws; the power of three, and Karma. What will you do with the rest of your time upon your planet? The choice is yours, dear one. For you will always have free will.*

*You will always have control, only for your life; your actions, your feeling and your thoughts.*

*Live in Love, Be in Love. Never expect another to do right by you, take the time and the presence to do the best you can do. Your life will be so much clearer when filled with Love and with Joy.*

*You are a perfect being of the Almighty Creator, you are whole, and you are loved. Be happy with the life you have chosen, and act accordingly to your own actions.*

*May Peace and Love forever be in your heart, just as it exists in your Soul.*

*Blessings,*
*~Archangel Metatron~*

## ~7 STEPS TO CONNECTING WITH YOUR GUARDIAN ANGEL~

Your Guardian Angel has been with you since God, the 'I AM', created your Soul. Your Soul in turn was given to this Angelic Being of Love and Light, helping you to transform into each life you take. Your Guardian Angel accompanies you through every step with an understanding, and a knowing about you intimately and completely. Their Love is completely *unconditional*.

Angels have the ability to increase your capacity to Love so that you become the loving energy which emanates from Creator. This loving energy comes in through your Crown Chakra and goes to your heart. This is a Love from an all-encompassing source, from the infinite, and is the purest, most everlasting Love in the Universe. It expands and it amplifies your abilities along with your willingness to share this Pure Love with others.

Angels have practical ways of guiding you to express your creative abilities and to help you increase the ability to express your Love to others. Angels do so by surrounding and grounding you, so that your work can be positive and effective with others, and within the Universe.

*Asking your Guardian Angel for help is your Divine right and a Divine privilege that results in powerful spiritual growth.*

## THE 7 STEPS:

**1) *Ask for help*** - Open yourself to Angelic Guidance. Allow yourself to be more receptive and allow the help to come through. When you diminish your receptivity, you limit the Angels ability to help you. When you create personal invocations, prayers, or mantras to call upon your personal Guardian Angel, you allow the Angels in to bringing you the help you need. You then open yourself up to greater acceptance of receiving in all areas of your life.

**2) *Connect your inner child*** - You are whole; you are innocent; you are a being of the purest of human Love. Your truths exist within you as you recognize Angels to be trustworthy gifts of your Creator. Your higher self; the inner child, will create an openness of receptivity and excitement, along with eagerness and wonder, preparing you to receive Angelic Gifts. Recognize that you *deserve* to have your Angels assistance in life, for guidance and direction upon your Soul's journey.

**3) *Give everything to Angels* -** By releasing all your worries and fears to the Angels they transmute this energy so that the results of your requests will come to you with your fullest desires at hand. Release any expectations from the Angels, as they know what is for your greatest and highest good.

**4) *ALWAYS Express Appreciation and Gratitude* –** It is always important in your life to find, and to ask, your Angelic guides to help you express a genuine appreciation and gratitude for things exactly as they are. To help you to find the Peace and Pureness of Love that is ever present in your heart. Have patience and let go of any expectations of how Love may be revealed to you. By showing Appreciation and Gratitude, you will raise your vibration of to that of one which carries happiness and understanding.

**5) *Know it is done* –** Every request you make is answered with the highest, purest of Love and Light. Guidance is *always* given to you. When there is fear that your request is not being answered, you block the Divine guidance from coming to you. ***Trust***, so that you will feel the Angel's Love in every prayer that is answered, or unanswered. Yes, unanswered; for unanswered prayers are blessings disguised in a way that may not be foreseen in your present mind. You are always loved completely and un-conditionally. Nothing that is less than your highest and greatest good shall be given to you. So it is a given that, *ALL* which serves you for your greatest and highest good shall never be withheld from you. You may just not recognize it.

**6)** *Act upon the received guidance* - Accept each opportunity as it shows itself to you in your life, and act upon it immediately. Angelic help is infinite and unlimited – you will not deplete its source; it is a well which will never run dry. There is no such thing as asking for "too much"; that simply does not exist, and the Angels give to you joyously; without limits.

**7)** *Celebrate yourself in the moment* - Give all your negative feelings about yourself, and your life, which expands to others, to the Angels for healing and transmutation. Allow them to release judgments and allow yourself to let go of everything that is not of a loving vibration. Surrender to the Angels, in the moment, and you will feel that you are able to accomplish more than you ever thought possible. Celebrate this deepened understanding of your Joyous relationship of Love that exists only between you and your Angel.

*All Angels are infinite and omnipresent,
and you can call upon any of them at
any time. Your request will not diminish
them in any way from their abilities,
or from their duties to help anyone else
who may need them, or who calls
upon them at the same time. Angels
exist beyond our experiences of time
and space so the will respond in accordance
to the Universal Laws, and so by
treating everyone as equal and
with complete unconditional Love.*

## ~ *METHODS THAT ANGELS MAY USE TO COMMUNICATE* ~

*Peo*ple have a tendency to think that all communication is like the movies will show ---- you see a vision of this magnificent Being and start to have a nice conversation! This is 'rarely' the case and therefore people sometimes get upset or discount their experiences until they drop their expectations of Angelic communication and begin to understand there are different methods and combinations of methods that the Angels use to get through to us.

There are endless ways that they may use to reach you! For me, I simply hear music, as it dances in the form of words in my head. And for me to understand what was being said to me, I asked for the gift of translation. Just like translating another language.

**VISUAL:** This is when you actually "see" the Angels and Masters, or you may be seeing symbols or pictures in your mind, or maybe around a person you are talking to. You may see something over and over again, put in your path by your Angel. In your meditations you see images that your Angel has sent you. They can be fragments, or follow a story line. Or you can see something ordinary and in that moment, it becomes overlaid with meaning. Or you may recall some memory from this life or a past-life that relates directly to what you are questing about. Colours can become very significant also. We tend to place an emotion with a color in a very personal way, so seeing a color "jump out at you" can be meaningful. The pictures may be like a slide show, rather than a movie.

Along with the gift of hearing the beautiful musical sounds of the Angels, I was blessed at times, especially during a healing session, I was able to 'see' the music, and still do, albeit not in the form of musical notes, but in the form of energy. It is truly a beautiful experience.

***AUDITORY:*** Have you ever heard a soft voice; it may sound a lot like yours, mostly though, it is an unfamiliar voice and may be accented. Music may be heard, before or during a message or music may *be* the message, like when some fragment of a tune may keep running through your head. Meditative, soul-vibration music can evoke feelings that prove to be quite accurate. You may compose or channel music, if you are so inclined. You may be "pushed" to turn on the radio at just the right time to hear a snatch of a song that has a message in it. People in our culture tend to be more open to music than many forms of communication. So, look for your message to appear in the form of a familiar song, one that may or may not have significant value, or memories to you. This is how the Angels will communicate with you. Through this song that will play inside your head. Listen to the message, love your personal Angel for bringing it to you in a way that you can understand.

***UNIVERSAL SYMBOLS:*** (Jungian, Gestalt, personal) These are your personal totems, including symbols, animals, etc. This type of communication can also include the use of various types of tools that utilize symbols, such as the Tarot, I Ching, Numerology, Runes, Astrological charts, etc. Nearly everyone has seen objects in clouds, curtains, walls, etc. Messages can be transmitted in this fashion. Symbols that we receive may be ones that "haunt" us for years and require the gradual unfolding and processing of years of work. Many in this era are seeing things like feathers in the most unlikely of places. This is a sure sign that your Angel is reaching out to you. Are you listening to the symbols you are finding? Are you finding dimes in the most unlikely of places, especially after you spend some time talking with your Angel? Try this; ask your Angel to show you a specific sign; something only significant to you, or the situation. Then wait. Your sign will appear, if you are paying attention. For me, I always ask for the sign to appear in sets of three.

***KINESTHETIC*** : you feel their energy field brush through or immerse yours (this can be subtle or profound). You may feel a touch on the shoulder, or elsewhere, depending on each person's receptivity to touch. This is a fairly common occurrence. Other common forms of kinesthetic communications include automatic writing, sculpting, painting, drawing, etc.

For me, my beloved 'Serena', my Guardian Angel, she has been known to outwardly 'slap' me in the back of my head. Now, Angels are NOT usually this aggressive. But my Angel knows what I need, and will use this measure on me when I am outwardly not paying attention to her. We have this agreement, because there was a period in my life, when I was ignoring her. Not deliberately, but with all the Angels that I communicate with on a daily basis, somehow, she was being missed, and perhaps a little thwarted by my behaviour. I make sure to listen to her, and when I don't, she lets me know!

You can have any relationship you want with your Guardian, it can be a silent one, or an overt one like I have with mine. It's up to you. But the Angels; your Guardian, is part of your life.

***VERBAL:*** This is when you open your mouth and you hear something amazing come out and you wonder "Where did that come from!?" When this happens, always remember to thank your Angel for giving you the wonderful things to say.

**DREAMS:** Your Angel will always speak to you through your dreams. Dreams need to be remembered to be of the most benefit to you, however. Therefore, it is NECESSARY to keep a dream journal, especially in the beginning. The dreams may be censored in some manner, protecting you from spiritual shocks by disguising the message. Your Angels may look different than they would at normal times, but you suspect, feel and/or "know" it is them, no matter how they show themselves to you in your dream. The way they look may have a direct bearing on where you are at in your life at the time of the message or dream. It can be quite comical or dramatic. They will go to great lengths at times to get your attention!

**OLFACTORY:** At times when you are communicating with your Guardian Angel, you may perceive an intense odor or fragrance that is closely associated with some feeling, memory or experience in the past or future. As an event unfolds, you may trigger where you smelled this odour before, and this may give you a much needed clue as to what is going on.

I remember at one very difficult time in my life, the intense odor of a bouquet of flowers. That is the best way to describe this to you, and it was only in one distinct spot in my bedroom, right in front of a portrait of my daughter and me. One step to the left, nothing. One step to the right, nothing. Shortly after that I got very ill. As I lay in my bed I smelt the scent again, accompanied by a soft touch to my cheek, and I fell asleep, and woke up perfect, no fever or chills; completely healed from what had ailed me.

***INTELLECTUAL/TELEPATHIC:***: This is when a seed of thought is "planted" in your mind and expands from the center of your mind, radiating into your awareness into your consciousness. It is a complete awareness, a 'knowing'.

***KNOWINGNESS***: This is the most common form of communication with your Guardian Angel. This can be difficult to explain when you haven't experienced it, but I am sure you have. The sense of 'knowing' is just that, Knowing. You don't know how, but you know that you know. This is closely related to the above method; Intellect/telepathic, because you simply have an absolute certainty about the event, question, situation, etc. You know exactly what the answer is, what action to be taken, etc. No one can convince you otherwise. People tend to underestimate the power and real elegance of this method.

***ACTUAL PHYSICAL PRESENCE***: This happens quite a bit, for most people, but you may not recognize them at the time! For most, this method will usually happen in unusual situations, or in emergencies, and not by all Angels. An Angel may appear in human form, and then be gone after helping you. Some have sightings of extreme Light appearing, and then it's gone. For me, it's all the time, and for those who know me, I see the Angels, your Angel, in the latter; its purest form, and that is as a Light source. Not any light, but the most beautiful colours of Light unlike any light anyone has ever seen. It is truly amazing. You too, when you practice working with your Angel, have the ability to see the Angels. But only when you are ready. And not all Angels will show themselves to you.

***THE FEELING OF A PRESENCE***: This type of awareness is quite important and needs to be mentioned. It is a very definite feeling of a "presence", an energetic quality. This may be accompanied by feelings of great Love emanating from the presence. This is often felt over a shoulder. Female energy is often over the left, male over the right, but this is not a hard and fast rule. This is also a very common form of experience. However, with more sightings of Spirits and Spirit Guardians, this method can be very hard to decipher at times. So it all comes down to how you are feeling when you feel, or even see the Angels. I say this because Angels will never make you feel uncomfortable, or scared. To see, or feel them you will encounter only feelings of great Love and Adoration.

**HIGHER SELF**: The Higher Self is a reflection of the Soul. It is the closest that we can come to our individual essence while we are still in our physical body. The Higher Self is the means we use to reach our Guardian. This is the ability to interact and communicate with our Guardian depends upon the clarity of the connection with our Higher Self; our Soul. That clarity and communication depends upon being *"centered"*. The integration with the Higher Self is a process of moving into and out of harmony with ourselves, over and over.

Sometimes it may seem as if we are *"in the flow"* with life, and everything is moving easily and effortlessly. At other times it can seem like we will never feel that ease again. This is a natural rhythm of life and as the saying goes: *"what goes up, must come down"*. Centering involves being grounded and connected with Mother Earth, breathing in her energies, while at the same time, being connected with the energies of the Universe by breathing in the energies of the Universal.

If you are in a time where your communication is just not happening, stop, give it a rest and know that it will start again. Be patient!! You may be overdoing it and need to take a break! Or you may not be centered.

As time goes on and your commitment is strong, you can move into the flow for longer periods of time.

*"WAKING DREAMS"* : This is a strange and wonderful way that your Angel will communicate with you. This involves having a symbol that is meaningful to you, one that serves as a link to your Angel and you. This works to increase your awareness, every day. Awareness of your surroundings, your feelings, thoughts, etc. It is an almost magical way that these methods come together for some people.

It can be a very simple event, such as meeting someone on a bus -- a total stranger -- you engage in a conversation and somehow, this communication is about the exact thing that was bothering you. The 'person' will suddenly leave and you end up feeling much better, musing to yourself about how nice that very conversation has helped you to get a better perspective on your situation, and then, there it was... Waking Dreams can be more complex, taking the form of a series of *'coincidences'* or happenings that give you information, warnings, reassurances; whatever you need for your spiritual growth. As I always say; *"There are no coincidences, a coincidence is your Angel stepping in!"*

After this encounter, start to pay attention to the information you receive, the signs/symbols you see or hear. As this will be your confirmation to your conversation with your Angel. It will always prove to be something valuable to your growth

*Don't expect your Angel to be able to do it all! You must walk through the doors that are opened for you; accept the help that is given. Remember, you have 'free will' in all that appens in **your** life. So you may be asking, but do you **believe**? Do you **trust**? All you really need when communicating with your Angel is three things; to **ask**, to **believe**, and to **trust**. And very importantly, ask that it be for your greatest and highest good, and the greatest and highest good for all. And, don't forget to say*
**"Thank-you"**!

## HEALING FEARS ABOUT ANGELIC COMMUNICATION:

Many people have various fears brought on by their upbringing, whether it be religion, or environment. It does not matter where the fear comes from; let's talk about these fears and how to heal them so that we may open ourselves up to Angelic communication.

\* The fear of seeing a frightening image. Ask *Archangel Michael* for support by saying:

> *"Archangel Michael, I ask that you enter into my mind, into my heart, and into my Soul to clean away all the effects of past mistakes in my thinking that may keep me from enjoying clear Spiritual sight."*

\* Fears left-over from childhood. Forgiveness of those who gave us the rules or those involved with our scary childhood prophecies.

\* Fears of breaking a 'rule' or incurring God's wrath. God has sent this Angel to us. Forgiveness of who gave the rules or those involved with our scary childhood prophecies.

\*The Fear of going crazy, dying, ascending or losing.

> *"Angels, please help me to open my window of clairvoyance so that I may once again see the truth and the beauty in your Love."*

* Fear of losing someone's love or approval if you open up to your clairvoyance. Help those around control (including becoming irresponsible) if you become clairvoyant.

> *"It is safe for me to be psychic; it is safe for me to see the truth; it is safe for me to see the future; it is safe for me to express my "true self". Unconscious mind, and higher self, I ask you to reveal to me the reasons why I have chosen you to understand their fears as you are learning more to understand your own."*

* Fear that you won't be able to see the Angels. The more anxious you feel about not being able to see the Angels will most likely increase your chances of not seeing them. Therefore, just learn how to relax and everything will come to you when you are ready.

## ~ *INCARNATED ANGELS, ELEMENTALS, WALK-INS AND STAR-PEOPLE* ~

*"Be careful when entertaining strangers, for by doing so, many have entertained Angel's Unaware"*
Hebrews 13:2

People have come from all over the Universe to live here on our planet Earth during this millennium shift. There are now so many extraterrestrials (ET's; Star People), Angels, and Walk-Ins on our planet right now.

Ultimately, we are all one. We are all one with the 'I AM' presence, with each other, with Angels, and with the Ascended Masters. Each one of us, individually, has the same Divine spark of God-Light within our core. Like multiple leaves attached to the same tree, we all have the same source, and it is because of this that we affect each other.

We appear to be separate beings, and have outward characteristics that distinguish us from each other. Both men and women have energies within us that are distinctly different from each other, and, depending on your lifestyle, you will have a different countenance and energy than someone who spends most of their time in a bar drinking. Your energy pattern will be affected by people you associate with, the thoughts that you think, and by the places you hang around in.

Not every child of the 'I AM' presence incarnates onto this Earth planet as the human Star-like Soul does. Some choose lives on other planes, or planets; their countenance and energy patterns will alternately affect their experiences and their surroundings. These energy patterns are then carried with them when they do choose to incarnate on the Earth.

In fact, many *'Light-Workers'* have had previous incarnations in other dimensions or planets and they have *chosen* to incarnate here on Earth at this time during this millennium shift.

In order for Angels and Star-People to adjust to this Earth life, they have 'borrowed' past-life memories from the Akashic records. These borrowed memories serve as buffers so that the Soul will know what to expect on this planet. Earth is considered to be the most violent, and volatile planet in which to incarnate to. The level of aggression on this planet is the highest of all the planets; in all the galaxies. Some of these beings are here to help the planet from destruction; others are here to bring Peace.

Not everyone who is an Incarnated Angel, Star-Person, Elemental, or Walk-In is here for the first time. Earth Angels may choose to come here repeatedly and they therefore retain the energy pattern of their realm of origin.

Let's take a moment now to talk about these different energies that are here on the planet. So we can understand, and maybe identify with one of these energies, just remember, not all of us here on this planet are from these categories.

***INCARNATED ANGELS*** - this group of incarnates have come here to this planet during this shift are here to help humans with the changes and challenges occurring at this time. Some common characteristics of these people are:

　****They look like Angels*** - they have sweet facial features, with heart shaped faces and childlike features, usually found in both men and in women. You will find that a very large percentage of the women will bleach or dye their hair blonde.

　****Relationship Challenges*** - these incarnates have a history of co-dependent and abusive relationships because of their predisposition to give and to nurture, always rescuing others. They see the *best* in everyone and therefore stay longer than the average person would in an abusive relationship. Incarnated Angels have a history of multiple marriages, divorces and co-dependent relationships.

***Compulsive Behaviours and Weight Issues*** - these incarnates have many compulsive behaviours to help them cope with being on the planet Earth. Especially overeating, they will turn to food to cope with their own emotional issues and are therefore quite often found to be overweight. Especially if they are disconnected with their own Spirituality.

***Professional Helpers and Healers*** - strangers often pour their hearts and personal problems out to these incarnated beings. Often feeling safe and secure in their presence. Therefore, you will find these beings in the health and healing professions, working where they can nurture their need to heal others. Nursing, social work, teaching; these are some of the professions you will find these beings in.

***Givers, NOT Receivers*** - very generous people, they often give without receiving; this often makes them feel very vulnerable. Subsequently, they can easily manifest great lack into their lives by blocking the flow of abundance, love, energy and other natural resources into their lives. Very sensitive to others needs and the feelings of others, Incarnated Angels often forget about their own needs and this can often lead to them having feelings of frustration and resentments.

*INCARNATED ELEMENTALS* - These groups of "Earth Angels" are here to help during the millennium shift, and are more commonly known as Elementals. Humans whose origins consist of those incarnates from the Elemental Kingdom, such as; Leprechauns, Sprites, Faeries, Brownies, and Elves. They can be mostly distinguished by:

*\*Celtic Heritage or Appearance* - they are often found sporting red or reddish-brown hair; fair skin; light-eyes; and Celtic Ancestry of Scottish, Irish, Welsh or British.

*\*They LOOK like Elementals* - Incarnated Elves, Brownies, or Leprechauns actually *look* like these characters we often find in children's books, both in body and in their facial features. Incarnated Faeries will often be found to be *willowy*, slender females who are moderately tall in height. It is very rare to see an overweight Faery.

*\*Characteristic Clothing* - Incarnated Elementals dress in clothing that is found to be typical of those types of Elementals. Faeries will dress in clothes that *flow*, while a Brownie will dress in heavily woven outfits, lacking in colour, comfortable shoes, typical to that of what a friar or a Monk would wear.

*\*Mischievous Personalities* - these particular incarnates can be found to be playful and jovial, sometimes to

the point of a passive/aggressive practical jokes. This characteristic comes from their dislike and distrust of humans.

***Alignment with Nature*** - these incarnated Souls have a Life Purpose to be aligned with, and to protect the Mother Earth and all her creatures who live upon her (with the exception of the humans). Elementals can easily be found in jobs that involve nature, plants and animals and should never work at jobs which confine them to the indoors.

***Manifesting Skills*** - these creatures are excellent sources of manifestation. They easily manifest their thoughts and experience results quickly in relativity. They can manifest massive wealth, *if* they put their minds to it. *However*, Incarnated Elementals who focus on pessimism can quickly manifest poverty just as easily.

**WALK-INS** - this is the third type of Earth Angel, commonly known as "Walk-Ins". These beings incarnate through a mutual agreement with a 'Walk-Out'; the human Soul of someone who wants to leave their position on Earth. This happens during a period of serious illness. And never happens while one is asleep. The Walk-In is a highly evolved Spiritual Being, with a Light-Worker's purpose to be upon the Earth. This transition usually happens quickly for the Walk-In has a need to bypass development as a fetus, being born and growing up. The Incarnate Soul locates a human who was not happy being alive. Perhaps this human is depressed, suicidal or having difficulty adjusting in this life.

The Walk-In Soul then communicates through dreams and meditation to the Walk-Out, and says "I will take over your responsibilities for you and you will be able to go home to Heaven, without any negative repercussions associated with suicide". If the Walk-Out agrees to vacate his/her body to allow the Walk-In full residency, then the two come to a mutual agreement, and a trial residency takes place before a permanent one. Swaps will happen several times before a final transition takes place. If everything goes smoothly, the Walk-Out then experiences, in the form of a life-changing incident such as a major accident or illness resulting in surgery for this final transition to take place.

At the agreed upon time, the transformation then takes place, and the Walk-In takes up permanent residency. A body can only house one Soul at a time, so after the transition, only the Soul of the Walk-In resides in the body. Everything is done with full permission and full co-operation of both parties; there are *no* negative or dark energies involved.

The Walk-In takes over full memories, and may not be aware that he/she is a Walk-In, since it can come from any incarnation. However, there are characteristics of the Walk-Ins life that are apparent:

***Drastic Personality Changes*** - immediately after the transition occurs. In fact, friends and family alike will remark at how the person is so different.

***Lifestyle Change*** - often the Walk-In does not like the Walk-Outs lifestyle and they begin to make changes such as divorce, change in jobs, bankruptcy, and even move to a different location. As part of the agreement though, the Walk-In must take care of the previous person's responsibilities; such as family and children, even during the transition. So, all lifestyle changes are handled as responsibly as possible.

***Name Change*** - after the transition is completed, the Walk-In may find that the Walk-Outs name is not appropriate to them, and does not suit them, so they may choose to change their first name, adopt a spiritual name or change their full name.

***STAR-PEOPLE*** - Are a group of individuals that come from many other planets from any of the planets, in any of the galaxies. They may Incarnate, or Walk-In. They are a higher evolution of individuals who have come to this planet for a variety of reasons. Most are here as a service to the planet Earth. They too have distinctive attributes that set them apart from others.

*****General boredom*** - many find it difficult to conform to the rules in society, they are often home schooled so that they are not bored in school, and can go at their own pace. As adults, they find themselves as bosses, or they will flounder from job-to-job throughout their life.

*****Misdiagnosed Disorders/Diseases*** - as children, many are given labels at a very young age. This can also contribute to their boredom. Often labelled with ADHD, ADD and Autism. These individuals are very unique within their own right. Brighter and smarter, they are here for a distinct purposes within our society.

So, when you look around you, know that everyone is not the same. Yes, we are all of the same source. We are all of the Creator, the 'I AM' presence; but we all come from a different place. Just as we all have an outwardly difference in appearance. Some have different skin colour, some different hair and eye colour. Know that it goes even deeper than that. 'Some', not all, are different Soul-beings. Nonetheless, we are all here for a Divine and unique purpose. Value your purpose, but more importantly, value one another's reason for being.

~ Blessed Be! ~

# HOW TO LIVE LIKE EARTH ANGELS DO

- ∞ Believe In Yourself!
- ∞ Believe You Have The Power To Change Things In Your Life
- ∞ Look Past The Obvious
- ∞ Look For The Inner Meaning Of Everything
- ∞ Trust Your Instincts
- ∞ Be Positive At All Times
- ∞ Be Peaceful
- ∞ Violence Is *Never* Necessary For Anything
- ∞ Feel Safe, Be Safe
- ∞ Do What Make You Happy
- ∞ Look To The Long Term
- ∞ Be Generous
- ∞ Do What You Think Is Right
- ∞ Stay Informed
- ∞ Network
- ∞ Be Sincere, Never Lie
- ∞ Fear Is An Illusion
- ∞ Try To Enjoy Everything You Do
- ∞ Enjoy Competition
- ∞ Don't Be A Sore Loser
- ∞ Eat Healthy Choices
- ∞ Drink Lots Of Water And Pure Juices
- ∞ Be Open, Be Honest
- ∞ Spend Time By Yourself Sometimes
- ∞ Hug, Read, Laugh, And Sing… A Lot!
- ∞ Show Your Appreciation, Always
- ∞ Travel When You Can
- ∞ Learn To Learn

- ∞ Don't Be Embarrassed
- ∞ Express Yourself
- ∞ Find Positive Motivation
- ∞ Celebrate Success
- ∞ Make Friends
- ∞ Listen To Music
- ∞ Apologize For Your Mistakes

# ~ *NUMBERS AND THE ANGELS* ~

Three or more of the same number (digital clock 2:22, 11:11, etc.). *Enhancing whatever level you are presently in.*

***111*** - Is the Energy flow of water, money, sex, and the kundalini. It's the magnetic experience that you feel when one of these energies manifests. This is known to be the universal number for Ascension. When you see multiples of the number 1, the Angels are telling you that you are succeeding in raising your vibrational levels to be closer to them.

***222*** - The Angels are telling you that whatever you are in the middle of in your life path, you are now entering into the process of resurrection of the process of ascension; the beginning of the 111 pattern.

***333*** ~ Body, Mind, Spirit; Mother, Maiden, Crone. Or, if you are Christian: Father, Son and Holy Spirit. The 333 pattern is the Trinity, the number to represent Spirituality. This is also a decision number, which means, that it is time for you to make a decision about your life. It is one thing to make a decision, but another to act upon it and make it happen. Either of the following may happen: 666 = material decision, or 999 = spiritual decision. You decide!

***444*** ~ This is the number that represents the Angels. Seeing this number lets you know that they are near you. They are trying to communicate with you; to let you know that you are not alone. Every time you see this number *'know'* that the Angels are close. Thank them! Feel their presence and feel their energy around you. If you take the time to feel their presence, you will feel the warmth of their energy as it engulfs you.

***555*** ~ This is the universal number of Harmony and Balance. The five characteristics of man: five fingers, five toes, five senses, and five limbs (two arms, two legs and the head). There are five bones forming the metacarpus, the metatarsal and the brain-pan. But most importantly, 5 brings you closest to the Divine Grace of the "I AM" presence that represents the Christ Consciousness; asking you to be aware of your Oneness with Creator. It tells you that you are a direct connection with the Universal Spirit and all its energies.

***666*** ~ This number has been linked to evil, but this could not be farther from the truth. This number represents a higher power of three (*Body, Mind & Spirit*); representing the material world and the chosen reality in which we live. As with the 333 number combination, this represents decisions that must be met in the material world.

***777*** ~ Symbolizes an integration of some portion of the four lower bodies with higher spiritual frequencies within the third-dimensional plane; or at level with which you are manifesting your physical reality on this Earth plane.

***888*** ~ Symbolizes infinity. *The unified spiral of the physical merging with the Spiritual*, thus moving you toward the completion and the ascension process through the energies of the 222 and 444.

***999*** ~ Symbolizes the last of the three levels of the trine (333, 666, 999), representing decisions that need to be met on the Spiritual plane; guiding you towards completion of your Soul's connection between the Earthly plane and the Universal plane.

***000*** ~ The *Great Void*. When seeing these numbers together, you are experiencing a 'null' zone; switching or moving you into a new energy field; a new life path. (11:11) Thus beginning a whole new level of development; another dimension or frequency of experience. This is your portal opening into the 12:12 of cosmic consciousness; your cosmic connection; your bridge to the future. This will signify a level of graduation, so pay attention to clocks, license plates, etc., as well as what you are doing, and thinking at the time you see this particular number configuration. I have found that seeing 000 to be very much a signal or sign after I have asked my Angels a question. Then, the answer appears.

# ~A BOX OF ANGELS~

*Supplies*:
- Construction paper
- Black marker
- List of affirmations/message
- Box
- Glue/paint/craft supplies
- Sheets of laminating plastic
- Hole punch
- Small angel stamp or stickers

*Instructions*:

* Cut construction paper into 2" by 3" slips. Decorate the strips with angel stickers (if you are inventive, you may want to cut the paper into the shapes of angels).

* With the black marker, write out one affirmation onto each paper.

* Laminate each piece of paper and punch a hole into each piece.

* Thread a piece of string or yarn in through the hole and tie.

* Decorate your box anyway you like and place the papers into the box. Pull out one of the affirmations each day and carry it with you!

**<u>Do this every day!</u>**

## ~ANGELIC MESSAGES TO USE EVERY DAY~

Love, within the being of one, is yours, take it, believe it. Be the essence of who you are, not what is being voiced to you that you should be.

~AA Metatron

Be honest with yourself and true to the path you have chosen. Walk accordingly; shine your light so that all may see.

~ AA Sandalphon

Be the light that you are. Recognize, acknowledge, and let go. Love and joy are the true essence of who you are and will live in your heart forever.

Many Blessings,
~ AA Uriel

---

The path to greater love is from within. It allows you to shine from within. Allow your vibration to rise and for you to show a greater light within.

~ AA Jophial

Release that of which you are not, embrace that which you are. See the beauty of life around you for it exists outside the chaos, and inside your heart. Inside you. You are the beauty of life. Living.

~AA Chamuel

Guidance is given unto you; it is your privilege and your right as a light of the Universe. You are the in control, and your love will guide you to that which is right. Know this, feel this; be one with thy self.

~ AA Grace

---

You are what you think, change the thoughts of your mind and know that you are perfect, complete and whole.

Release all that is keeping you from your future, your true happiness; the joys of the present that you hold toward

True happiness and joy are within you. The trueness of your essence is for you to enjoy and for you to live completely and

| | | |
|---|---|---|
| You are a shining light of the creator.<br><br>Blessed Be<br>~ AA Zadkiel | your future. You cannot change that which has gone.<br>Blessed be the future of your present.<br>~ AA Radzekiel | fully to be the most you can; live love and laugh.<br><br>Blessed Be<br>~ AA Chamuel |
| Find the truth in your heart and the trueness of your soul can be freed with enlightenment.<br><br>~ AA Raziel | Life's experiences happen; Your experience happens. You are the one in your life who will decide all which you will experience. Embrace life. Live. Love.<br><br>~ AA Uriel | Trust that you will find that which makes you happiest. Your pure purpose comes to you with love and faith and we are guiding your way; just open your heart.<br><br>~ AA Tatiana |
| Embrace thyself and love wholeheartedly. Change that which does not work and love that which does. Happiness lies within.<br><br>~ AA Ramiel | Create all that is wonderful, all that is beautiful, each experience is an enlightenment into all that is you. All that you are. All that you will become.<br><br>~ AA Raziel | Guide your Essence to the light of your future. The light of your path. The essence of your Soul, of your trueness of love and light within you.<br><br>~ AA Raziel |
| Be true to that which lies within the heart and your joy will reveal itself on your path going forward into your life as it is | Allow your greatness to shine, look in the eyes that are value in your life. In those eyes your greatest attributes will shine. You will see your | What colour is your light as it shines its freshness upon the landscape of your life?<br>Create your landscape of colour |

| | | |
|---|---|---|
| meant to be lived.<br><br>Blessings,<br>~ AA Ariel | greatness.<br><br>Blessed Be<br>~ AA Muriel | onto the world.<br>Spread greatness of love and joy to all.<br><br>~ AA Sandalphon |
| You can free your heart of pain if you allow yourself to see and to connect within you to that which lights your soul.<br><br>~ AA Raziel | Live, Love, Laugh…<br>Be the life you want to live. Be the Joy within your heart. Claim the life that is yours.<br><br>~ AA Gabriel | When you speak, speak from the heart.<br>When you listen, listen with your heart. All is not which it seems. Behind each person is expression.<br><br>~ AA Radzekiel |
| Don't lose the memories of who you were, allow them to mould into that which you are, to form a new you that you will become. Honour that place within you, that is you! You are Love.<br><br>~ AA Sandalphon | You are not one person in this vast complex universe, although, you are one complex being filled with the love, and joy of the one source light.<br>Be true to yourself, rise above your fears to the light that which you are.<br><br>~ AA Raziel | Know who you are and trust your greatest gift; you have access to all your deepest desires. Reach for your Soul, and achieve all that you desire in this lifetime.<br>Nothing can stand in your way but you!<br><br>~ AA Radzekiel |

| | | |
|---|---|---|
| *You are wonderful, you are incredible, your light shines throughout the world. Peace lives in your heart, in your Soul, and is to be shared.*<br><br>*~ AA Raziel* | *There is greatness within you. You are whole, you are perfect, you are one of the chosen ones.*<br><br>*Blessed be*<br>*~ AA Metatron* | *This is your life, be responsible in your own being, to your path. For that is the journey, that is the destination.*<br><br>*~ AA Raziel* |
| *In the light of the morning, go within and let your true light shine. You are beautiful and perfect, and I love you!*<br><br>*~ AA Radzekiel* | *You will receive the blessings of the Divine to fulfill the purpose you have set out to receive in this lifetime. With great peace in Love and in Light.*<br><br>*~ AA Raziel* | *Bring balance into your life, certainty will prevail, and everything will come to be as it should be.*<br><br>*Many blessings,*<br>*~AA Metatron* |
| *Love is in your heart, light your way to a brighter future and a happier life. You are perfect, you are whole, live a happier, more fulfilled life.*<br><br>*~ AA Metatron* | *Live your life as you are meant to. All is yours when you are living in the light. Many blessings of love.*<br><br>*~ AA Chamuel* | *The life you choose to live is your own. Be happy, be the love you are, and the love you want to give. I love you all.*<br><br>*~ AA Jophial* |
| *Everything in your life has its purpose,* | *Bloom from the love in your heart. All* | *You are the power within you; feel love* |

focus on yours and life will blossom forward.
Honour thyself.

~ AA Radzekiel

that will be, will be and you are still loved. You exist as a spiritual being on this planet; I love you, just as you are.

~ AA Radzekiel

in your heart so that you may find the ultimate happiness within you. Pure Love and Pure Light are you.

~ AA Zadkiel

---

You are many things, many beautiful things. And I love you for who you are. Not what you have become. You are a wonderful Soul of Love and Joy.

~ AA Uriel

Listen with your heart. Be at one with the ways of the spirit.
Allow the voice to move within you and you will be able to clear away debris.

~ AA Cathetel

We shine down upon you to guide you to help one another. To help another, you must first shine within yourself.

~ AA Camael

---

Know that everything that is your happiness is you!!! Create with the greatest power ~ YOU ~ You are the most wonderful Soul there is... be ALL that you can be.

~ AA Gabriel

Be the peace in your heart and the joy in your soul. Live life one moment in time. Expressing love at the deepest level of self; you will feel change. Peace.

~ AA Radzekiel

Each moment of each day is full of wonderment, if you just look to the moment with your heart. Love for today.
Live for the magic.

~ AA Raziel

---

Look deep within, your heart it feels

Shine within all that which has been

You are perfect in every way. Life does

| | | |
|---|---|---|
| *wonderful, and joyful. Embrace it; live life fully in the moment.*<br><br>*~ AA Chamuel* | *bestowed upon you, feel life as you live it in each moment and each experience.*<br><br>*You are life; you are the flower that blooms, bringing joy to all that see it.*<br><br>*~ AA Michael* | *not define who you are. You are the most important soul in your life. Simply love yourself…as I love you!*<br><br>*~ AA Chamuel* |
| *Be the person you are truly inside, allow life to shift and change for wondrous things are upon you.*<br><br>*~AA Radzekiel* | *Love and joy are the true essence of who you are and will live in your heart forever.*<br><br>*~AA Uriel* | *You are a light received by many. Shine your light and be at peace.*<br><br>*~AA Raziel* |

# ~ANGEL WRITING MEDITATION~

*Take a moment, and fully read this meditation before you begin. You may want to make a recording of this meditation. Or you can contact Angelyn Joy for your digital recording of this meditation through her website: www.mysticangel.wordpress.com;*

Find a place where you won't be disturbed, and where you can be comfortable for lying, or sitting, for an extended period of time. Make sure all phones are turned off so that you can be comfortable, and warm. Set the atmosphere so you can relax. ~ e.g. candles, flowers, incense, etc. Have a glass of water close by and some paper and pencil to record your experiences.

Begin by taking a couple of slow, deep breaths, making sure to breathe in through your nose and out your mouth. Three slow deep breaths. This will help to lower your vibration and still your mind and body to bring yourself to relax fully.

Visualize yourself in a beautiful glass conservatory, with windows all around you. The ceiling is a beautiful domed shape of glass, allowing the light to shine through. The floors are a polished white marble that reflect the sun as it shines in. You feel as if this conservatory is standing on top of a hill, because all you can see around you is beautiful blue skies, and fluffy white clouds.

Imagine that you are sitting on a beautiful, velvet couch and that there are other chairs set out with little white tables, and on top of each of the tables are pretty vases of fresh flowers and cool drinks. On one of the tables you notice a beautifully decorated notebook and pencil.

Double doors stand before you, at the other end of the room. You can see the path which winds down the hill. And all around you, you can see the sunlight and blue skies. A cool breeze blows in through these doors making this a pleasant and relaxing place to be. Rest. Breath in the beautiful clear air. The atmosphere of this room is peaceful and calming. Feel the sun on your face.

You are aware of the beautiful blue sky. There are soft wisps of cloud like images that appear, and move all around you. They appear in soft iridescent colours of the rainbow. While you can't touch them, you know they are real. You know they are beings of Light - Angels.

Relax deeper into the sofa, feeling the cushions embracing your body as you fall deeper into a state of pure relaxation. Falling as a leaf falls from a tree; gently blowing into the breeze. You are molded into the cushions as they protect you.
~ Close your eyes... without words, ask your Guardian Angel to be near you. Wait - relaxing and feeling as if you are floating. Gently now... open your eyes. There is a beautiful light gliding through the double doors. You see the Image of your Angel. Invite them in. Listen to what they have to share with you. Ask your Angel anything you wish. Be sure to write down everything your Angel tells you.

When you are done, remember to offer your Angel Gratitude and thanks for being with you today. Close your eyes, and take a few deep breaths... when you open them you will again be on your own. Spend a moment in the room, embracing the feeling of Peace, Serenity and Relaxation.

When you are ready, allow your conscious mind to float back to you, allowing you to fade away from this beautiful place; knowing fully that you can return to it again anytime you wish.

Allow each breath you take to now bring you back into reality... into your present place... and into your consciousness.

Take a deep breathe, as you become fully aware of your surroundings.

Take another deep breathe and allow yourself to slowly open your eyes. Bring a smile to your face and say *"thank you"*.

When you are fully awake and fully aware, take some time to reflect on the visit with your Angel. Make your own notes to remember this experience with your Angel.

*** Blessed Be,***
*** ~Archangel Radzekiel~***

## ~ *About the Author* ~

*Born in the metropolis of Toronto on the third day, of the third month in the sixties, Angelyn spent most of her formative years in and out of hospitals, causing much concern for her parents and her family; resulting in a quiet, withdrawn child. What those around her didn't know, was that beyond the surface, something wonderful was meant to happen in this child's adult life that would have an impact on the world around her and the people's lives that would be touched. All that she had become, and all that she was going through, was to prepare her for her for what was to come.*

*What happened in her thirties, something that could have been detrimental, ended up being something wonderful. In the late 1990's, Angelyn encountered several encounters with cancer, leading to operations, and struggles. As a single mom, she had no choice but to 'muddle' through. In 1999, her life changed. She made the decision to take charge of her life, her world, and her dis-ease. Her journey then began with the healing of her body, mind, and spirit.*

*As she went to various healers, Angelyn also took courses to open up her soul, to truly become one with herself and the world around her. During this new journey, Angelyn discovered that the lights and sounds that were always a part of her life were something truly magical, and wonderful - Angels. They were not only there to help her to heal, and to help her on her journey, but she was in fact, one of them. It was on this journey that she learned of her soul name: Radzekiel. The Archangel Radzekiel.*

*With this information, Angelyn became engrossed in Meditations to truly understand who she was and who her brethren were. Intense conversations with the Angels led Angelyn to be able to channel the Angels, and to translate their words for others. Her gift enabled her to transform these images onto paper for others to see and connect with their Guardians.*

*During this time, Angelyn was able to create workshops, and become the teacher she always dreamt she would be. This book is based on one of those workshops.*

*Angelyn has written many healing articles on spirituality and appeared on many television programs and radio programs talking about her experiences with the Angels. Angelyn travels all over North America talking to others about recognizing and connecting with their own personal Guardian Angel, and all the Angels they have access to on a daily basis.*

*Angelyn is a world renowned Angelologist, Reiki Master, Aromatherapist and Psychic; spreading her healing love and the voices of the Angels all around the world. You too can experience Angelyn's gifts through her website: mysticangel.wordpress.com or on Facebook: www.facebook.com/angelyn4joy. She will be happy to share her experiences with you, or help you connect with your own personal Guardian.*

*Watch for up and comong books from Angelyn. Her first book* **"Messages from the Light"** *is a compilation of some of the messages shared with Angelyn from the Angels and can be purchased at www.lulu.com.*

## ~Namaste~

CPSIA information can be obtained
at www.ICGtesting.com
Printed in the USA
BVOW03s2320070717
488728BV00001B/21/P

9 781312 444973